In Life—in Death— He Leads

Bruce Blair

WestBow
PRESS
A DIVISION OF THOMAS NELSON

WestBow Press books may be ordered through booksellers or by contacting:

WestBow Press
A Division of Thomas Nelson
1663 Liberty Drive
Bloomington, IN 47403
www.westbowpress.com
1-(866) 928-1240

Scripture taken from the Holy Bible, New International Version®. Copyright © 1973, 1978, 1984 Biblica. Used by permission of Zondervan. All rights reserved.

Scripture taken from the King James Version of the Bible.

Scripture taken from the New King James Version. Copyright 1979, 1980, 1982 by Thomas Nelson, inc. Used by permission. All rights reserved.

Scripture taken from the International Standard Version of the Holy Bible.

ISBN: 978-1-4497-9423-1 (sc)
ISBN: 978-1-4497-9422-4 (e)

Library of Congress Control Number: 2013908040

Printed in the United States of America.

WestBow Press rev. date: 05/07/2013

Table of Contents

Prologue

There are two reasons why I wrote this book. Because I have been given so many precious experiences, it is my duty and honor to share my story, to inspire you in your spiritual walk, to lead those searching for answers to life's big questions, and to glorify our Lord and Savior, Jesus Christ. The Bible says that we should tell our children and their children, right on down the line, about the great miracles that Jesus has performed in our lives. God performed miracles for the children of Israel, and He is still performing miracles today. Jesus Christ is the same—yesterday, today, and forever. I believe my life experience is strong evidence that God does exist and intervenes in our lives.

> Therefore you shall lay up these words of mine in your heart and in your soul, and bind them as a sign on your hand, and they shall be as frontlets between your eyes. You shall teach them to your children, speaking of them when you sit in your house, when you walk by the way, when you lie down, and when you rise up. (Deut. 11:18–19)

Second, I wanted to pass on my family history to the new generations in my family. The project all started the day I thought about how little I knew of my ancestors. I didn't know anything about my grandfathers. What were they like? What were their hopes and fears? Were theirs anything like mine? The world is changing faster with each successive generation. I suspect that my grandchildren will be more inquisitive about me than I was about my grandparents. God led me and my family through some very tough situations, including when I had a glimpse at life after death, hence the name of my book: *In Life, In Death, He Leads.*

God's Warnings for This Generation

Our once Christian nation has been poisoned by secularism. I think the timing of this book may align with the concerns of the times in which we live. God is using many means to give us a warning. As I look at today's news, it seems that America has decided that we no longer need our Creator or Savior. It is troubling to know that our elected officials take their oaths to defend the Constitution with one hand on the Bible. While some of these leaders know what power it contains, so many others don't and won't support Christian beliefs. Job's friends describe the wicked as:

> They spend their days in wealth, And in a moment go down to the grave. Yet they say to God, 'Depart from us, For we do not desire the knowledge of Your ways. Who is the Almighty, that we should serve Him? And what profit do we have if we pray to Him?' (Job 21:13-15 NKJV)

Our founders asked God to look over us and guide us as a new nation. I believe this invocation ("a petitioning for help or support") happened in a little chapel just across the street from the World Trade Center. Do you remember when the World Trade Center came down on 9/11 and a sycamore tree was knocked down so that it rested upon the little chapel as if to protect it? The chapel survived nearly unscathed. God has given us the prophecy in Isaiah 9:9-15 and in other Scriptures to show us how He feels about our ignoring His warnings.

> And all the people shall know, even Ephraim and the inhabitant of Samaria, that say in the pride and

stoutness of heart, the bricks are fallen down, but we will build with hewn stones: the sycomores are cut down, but we will change them into cedars. Therefore the LORD shall set up the adversaries of Rezin against him, and join his enemies together; The Syrians before, and the Philistines behind; and they shall devour Israel with open mouth. For all this his anger is not turned away, but his hand is stretched out still. For the people turneth not unto him that smiteth them, neither do they seek the LORD of hosts. Therefore the LORD will cut off from Israel head and tail, branch and rush, in one day. The ancient and honourable, he is the head; and the prophet that teacheth lies, he is the tail. (Isa. 9:9–15)

The Bible has recorded how God's people went into captivity over and over again because of their defiance of God. As a nation, we are following in their exact footsteps. One night I dreamt about the destructive winds being held back by four angels in the Book of Revelation.

After these things I saw four angels standing at the four corners of the earth, holding the four winds of the earth, that the wind should not blow on the earth, on the sea, or on any tree. (Rev. 7:1)

It seems that the winds are being unleashed in seven-year cycles between the great destructive storms Katrina and Sandy, the national crisis of 9/11, and the housing market collapse of 2008. Shouldn't we be taking God's warnings seriously? As a nation, we need to open our eyes and hearts and acknowledge God. On several occasions our leaders have pronounced our own judgment when they said we will rebuild bigger and better; we will plant the cedar tree where the Lord blew down the sycamore.[1] Could it be that America is at that place where judgment is occurring? God said, "Thou fool, this night thy soul is required of thee!" If God allowed all of these things to happen as a warning to us about taking God and the Bible out of our national conscience, then I wonder if somehow God has already given us His final warning of our coming destruction.

Considering the way in which the Devil and perhaps the Antichrist are working today, there may not be a Bible for our grandchildren to read. However, the way of eternal salvation is made clear in my stories. My prayer is that you, the reader, will be blessed and made whole by Jesus.

—*Bruce Blair*

---

[1] Cahn, Jonathan. *The Harbinger: The Ancient Mystery that Holds the Secret of America's Future*. Lake Mary, Florida: FrontLine, 2012.

CHAPTER 1

The Beginning

My father was born in 1892. He had two brothers and a sister. His family was from Kentucky; Mom's was from Wisconsin. Dad was a gentle man who loved his family. My parents had a wonderful marriage and rarely argued. If harsh words ever came out, they were saved for another day and another place. Dad was a hard worker, and in those days things were not easy; you had to work for what you got. Mom and Dad were generous and always willing to help those in need. Although they didn't have money to give, if you came by and were hungry, they fed you. They farmed in Charles Mix County, South Dakota. From there they moved to a ranch about three and a half miles west of Oelrichs, South Dakota. There were six of us children, Helen, Lorraine, Donald, Bob, Bruce, and Shirley. I was number five. My brother Bob was fifteen months older than I and was my constant companion for about the first fifteen years of my life.

Early Memories

Although I was younger than four years old before we moved west, some events have stuck with me through the years. There was a double granary on the farm. In the center of each end was a door that had openings to allow a car or truck to enter. Dad had a hired man who parked his car in there. Bob and I found a bucket of old oil and some brushes, and we decided it would be a good thing to paint that car. The oil made it nice and shiny, and we didn't think we were doing anything harmful.

In that same granary, I was the lucky finder of an old milk of magnesia bottle that had something in it. With a little effort and some ingenuity on my part, I got the lid off. It just looked like water, and of course with my shaking it up good, spilling it all over my little bib overalls and down on my bare feet, I was having a ball. Little did I know that it was battery acid. Soon my feet began to burn; I was in trouble, so I began to cry. Bob was always a good sympathizer, and if I cried, he'd join me. By the time Mom found us, and the problem, the acid had eaten into my foot so that I carried a scar for a number of years. There wasn't much left of my little overalls.

In my earliest recollections, there is a picture in our house of a small boy and girl on a rickety wooden bridge with an angel watching over them. It doesn't take much imagination to see that an angel was watching over a little boy spilling acid on himself.

The Storm Cellar

Ours was tornado country. One stormy evening, Bob and I were wakened and taken to the underground storm cellar. On this occasion the storm that came up so fast that our parents didn't have time to get everybody into the cellar soon enough. My grandfather and the rest of our family got into the cellar; my father was out in the fields and came in as soon as he could after putting the horses in the barn. The storm was coming on fast, and when Dad tried to enter the cellar, he pulled the latch, but no matter how hard he pulled, it would not open more than a few inches. My grandfather had hold of the door on the other side and thought that the storm was lifting the door, so with increased effort he would pull it closed again. This went on with renewed vigor on both sides until my dad finally pulled so hard that he almost lifted my grandfather out of the cellar. This was cause for much laughter.

The Depression

The year 1929 was a dark time. Banks failed and the stock market crashed. Dad had a good corn crop that year, but it wasn't worth picking because there was no market for it. The people who lived through those times were imprinted the rest of their lives. We always knew that my dad was fearful of a repeat. He had six kids to feed and clothe. This is when we made the big move out west.

My grandfather was a good businessman. In the preceding years, he was able to purchase three farms, so when the Depression hit, we moved three hundred miles west and lived on one of them. One of Dad's brothers and his sister also moved west. We always had a few milk cows, and our lives revolved around them. The first thing we did in the morning was milk them. That took at least an hour. Then the milk had to be separated. We had a manual separator that needed to be cranked at approximately the same speed at all times or else the cream would come out too thick or too thin. Skimmed milk would run out of one spout and into milk buckets. The skimmed milk was then fed to the calves in their pen.

The cream would run out of the other spout, directly into a five- or ten-gallon cream can. Our refrigeration method was to use the snow-filled cistern. The cream would be set in a cool place until the can was full and ready to ship. In the summer, on cream shipping day, we would wait until the train was almost ready to depart before taking the can down to the depot so as to avoid the hot sun, which would otherwise spoil the cream. This was a special time for me. The old monster steam engine would be snorting steam and shaking the earth as she rolled in. After the train left, we'd go home and enjoy a wonderful breakfast, often pancakes with whipped cream.

After Dad was born again—that is, after he received Christ—our folks set up a time after breakfast for morning worship. This was a time when we would read the Bible and then kneel, taking our turns coming to the Lord in prayer. At my young age, this meant very little to me, but it was the beginning of learning discipline and obedience. I knew that there was a God who knew all about and cared for me, and I believed that I should do all I could to stay on His good side. Mom was the law, the jury, and the one who meted out the punishment. Dad shaved with a straight razor, and the leather strop he used to sharpen it hung on the wall as a reminder that lawbreakers would be swiftly and surely punished. It is amazing how well the system worked in those days.

Every year we would send off to the hatchery for five hundred baby chicks. We kept a few hogs. In the wintertime we would get together with Uncle Claude and butcher several pigs or a steer. What with the chickens, milk, and cream, we all forgot that we had very little.

In the summer we would go without shoes, which was fine with us since we thought shoes were a nuisance. Being almost poor didn't bother us except for once, during a situation that came up at school. I was cast as an angel in the Christmas play. In order to get my wings and costume on, I had to nearly undress in front of the teacher. The problem was that as the youngest boy in my family, by the time the long johns got to me, they were usually full of holes. The teacher knew that we had so little, but to my mind I would have gladly taken a walloping over having her see me in those "holey" underwear.

When I was around twelve, Dad gave me a chance to handle teams of horses. I could harness the horses and handle them pretty well. Once, my four-horse team was pulling four sections of harrow, and I was walking behind doing the driving. I got down to the end of the row and had to rest the horses for a while. When I got ready to go to work again, I noticed that the three-year-old horse had gotten his bridle off, and I was too short to get it back on him; he would raise his head out of my reach. Anyway, he got nervous and jumped his front feet up onto the horse next to him. That is when the excitement started. It was just like a chain reaction. One horse scared the other, and they all took off. I was helpless to do anything but get out of the way. My heart sank inside my chest as I watched them go over the hill on a dead run. Bob and Don were over the hill hoeing weeds. Imagine the awe on their faces when they saw the team coming over the hill at full gallop. By the time those horses stopped, they had torn up the harrow and most of the harness. Dad spent several days just repairing the harness, and he decided then that I was just too short and would have to grow a little taller before I could do any more of that fieldwork.

Dad purchased an old buggy with springs that was like a car; it had a spring seat to sit in. I was able to harness up the older team of horses and hook them to this buggy. One day I was going down a hill in full gallop when the tongue of the buggy came loose from the neck yoke and dropped to the ground. It stuck into the ground, lifting the front of the buggy as it went under. I suppose it threw me at least fifteen feet into the air, seat and all. When I came to my senses, the horses had stopped and were just standing there. The buggy was tipped over and had made a mess. I brought the horses to the side and let them pull the buggy back onto its wheels and straighten things out so I could continue on my way. The fall should have broken my neck, to say the least. Again, my guardian angel had to have been there to break my fall somehow.

But there were bright spots in life, too. I especially remember the Christmas of 1935. The "bear-tooth hold" that the plagues of locusts, hailstorms, dust storms, etc., had on the country seemed to relax a little, and we had a fair crop that year. In those times, Montgomery Ward and Sears, Roebuck and Company would always send us their mail-order catalogs. From the time the catalogs came into our homes, we pored over just about every page. It seemed like those stores sold everything that a person could desire. It didn't take us boys long to pick out the desires of our hearts—that year, high-laced boots and pretty gray socks with the red stripes that would fold down over the tops of the boots. To top it all off, we definitely wanted a little pocket sewn onto the side of one boot in which to carry a jackknife. Christmas morning came for Bob and me, and our prayers were answered. We each got a little box with a four-bladed Scout knife inside. It didn't take us long to find some strips of leather and braid them together so we could tie our knives to ourselves and avoid losing them. It was a happy Christmas even though we didn't get the boots with the jackknife pockets sewn on.

Skunks and Sin

My oldest brother Don was four years older than I and, as it turned out, quite an entrepreneur. When one of his friends told him how he'd dug out a den of sixteen skunks and sold the pelts, it didn't take Don long to realize that sixteen times any amount from $2.00 to $4.50 a pelt would make him rich. Don set a goal to turn skunk pelts into cash, and I was to be part of that plan. We had walked about three miles to an old, unoccupied house and determined that there was likely at least one skunk under it. This house didn't have a foundation the likes of which we know today. It sat on large stones placed every six to eight feet so you could see all the way through. Because of the unevenness of the ground, one end of the house was right down on the ground, and the skunks had made a cozy little nest there for the winter. Since I was the smallest, Don made me a deal that I couldn't refuse. He told me that he would pay me ten cents to crawl under and poke at the skunks in the nest with a stick and drive them toward him, where he would club them. I agreed to this, with dreams of what I'd do with the money that was surely coming my way. I got the skunk pushed out of his nest, and I headed him toward the prearranged exit. It looked like money in the bank until the skunk figured out that there was an execution party waiting outside the safety of the house, so he turned around and shot me in the eyes. My eyes were burning, and I reeked of this horrible odor that I feared would be permanent. I threw down the stick and quit. My brother could see his profits going down the drain, so he made me another offer of twenty-five cents. By now my eyes were not burning so badly and I was getting used to the smell, so after a lot of coaxing on Don's part, I decided to try again, dreaming of what all that money would buy. Needless to say, the outcome was the same, and all we went home with were my burning eyes and a "perfume" nobody wanted.

When sin comes into our lives, it is kind of like when that skunk shot me in the face. It stung my eyes and the smell was stifling, but after a while it didn't seem so bad, so I went in again to try to get the skunk out. When you first sin, it seems so bad and it really stinks, and you wonder why you would have ever thought of doing such a thing. Then later you commit the same sin again, and this time it doesn't seem to smell so bad. The next thing you know, you can continue in that same sin and it doesn't seem to smell as bad.

War and Evil

It was in the late 1930s when Hitler was coming into power, and, as children, we knew that communism had to be about the worst thing that could appear on the face of the earth. It was also the time of John Dillinger, the notorious criminal known for his tommy-gun killings. TV hadn't been invented yet, so Dad would listen to the radio for the news, and we could occasionally get episodes of *Amos 'n' Andy.* We also learned about the war in Ethiopia where lye, intentionally dumped on the ground, was eating people's feet. We could not believe that people would do such a thing to each other. Today, by the time a child gets to grade school, he or she has heard about thousands of murders, seen the inhumane treatment of others, and been witness to immoral living[2]. God is telling us that there are consequences to sin; we know that deep down. We are reaping today, as we see parents who will not correct their children. Unless we repent, I believe that we are in the very last days of this earth's existence.

God Reached Out to Dad

It was up to Mom to get us ready to go to church. Dad didn't go, so when we children could, we got out of it. Many times Mom won the argument and carted us off to church. It was during one of these times that the Lord sent a preacher to our town. He was very funny. When we'd come home laughing, Dad would ask us what the preacher had said. This finally aroused Dad's curiosity, and he started going to church with us to see for himself what was so funny. Conviction for his sin set in, and it wasn't long until my dad was born again. I sure didn't understand what had happened, but I could see that my dad was a happy man. He would go around singing about it all the time. "O happy day, happy day, when Jesus washed my sins away." I guess I wasn't old enough to comprehend what really happened, but I was glad.

My Time As a Young Man

In 1940 we had a really good corn crop. By then I was the only boy left at home. My dad and I picked the corn by hand, and I learned what work really was. The corn never got too tall, so I had to bend over to pick it then throw it into the wagon. After picking a load, I had to unload it with a shovel. I was sure that my back would break.

---

[2]   Norman Herr, Ph.D., Prof. of Science Education., California State University, Northridge, *Internet Resources to Accompany The Sourcebook for Teaching Science*, Section III Violence.

To this day, I have great respect for workers who have to bend over to pick crops.

The following year my parents sent me to Colorado for a year of Bible school. I am sure that the Lord was doing everything that He could to get me to straighten out—it just didn't take. My mind at this time was just not able to comprehend what it was all about.

The next few years went by fast. A year or so before I enlisted in the service, I was working in a dairy where my brother-in-law also worked. One afternoon, after we were done milking, I got into my 1930 Chevy and hollered to my brother-in-law that I could beat him home. He had a 1937 Ford pickup, and I knew that I would need a head start in order to beat him. I was staying with him and my sister, so we had the same destination. As soon as he heard me, he took off in a run to get to his truck and get in the race. There were little knolls in the road that you couldn't see over until you were right on top of them. The neighbor boy had just begun to drive his milk cows out of the pasture and toward the barn. He had them crossing the road. He had left his horse and buggy in the ditch while he closed the gate. I popped over the hill, and all I could see were those cows and no way through them. My old car only had one rear wheel that would lock up for brakes. When I saw the cows, I was approximately one hundred and fifty feet from them. As I slid through that herd, I had a vision of the wooden frame of the car splintering. When I got through the cows, my legs were shaking so badly that I had to pull out the hand throttle to keep going. My brother-in-law made it through right behind me, and neither of us ever touched a cow! I believe that the same guardian angel that was watching over my brother and me was there, and that was how my brother-in-law made a way through the cattle. My brother-in-law went into the mission field in Haiti for thirty years. I'd love to talk to that boy who was taking his cattle home and ask him what he saw that day.

Military Service

I enlisted in the Navy soon after I reached eighteen years of age. Our country was still at war with Germany, and the battle with Japan was far from over. I really enjoyed the service. I don't know if it was just getting away from the farm or the new experiences. I think the first serious thought I had was when I was aboard a ship and we went under the Golden Gate Bridge, heading for the South Pacific. For some reason as I looked back on that Golden Gate Bridge, I felt that I'd never see it again. For this little farm boy, it was the trip of my life.

There were many exciting times. One time we were in a thirty-six-ship convoy from New Guinea to the Philippine Islands, and there was a report that a submarine was after us. The destroyers in our convoy were dropping depth charges to try to protect us. When it was all over, we were still afloat and in very dangerous waters, as the Japanese still held some islands that were not too far away. We had planes flying over us for several days while we were in the most dangerous area.

As we came back north across the equator, it seemed like the water turned an angry green. As I write this, I can still feel the throb of the engines coming up through the steel deck and the warm tropical breezes blowing in my face as darkness was coming on. Even in the peace of the moment there was always that foreboding feeling of the night's coming. Bad things happened in the dark of night. We knew that at any minute we could be hit by a torpedo and all become shark bait. We finally got to our destination, the Gulf of Leyte in the Philippine Islands. This area was to be my home for sixteen months.

On our way over, the Germans had been defeated, but it wasn't over with the Japanese. We had gone ashore, and I was to be in a receiving station until I was assigned somewhere. It wasn't long until the air-raid siren went off and we headed for cover. I'll never forget the feeling that went through me at that time. The only way to describe it is with the word *fear*. I had never known real fear until then.

Time moved quickly, and I nearly learned the local language while I was there. The islands were beautiful to my eyes. My job was to chauffeur the military "brass," picking them up at the airport and taking them around on inspections. So, I was able to see different parts of the island. I had never been exposed to the high surf that would roll in on the west side of the island before; truly, it was the most beautiful blue that I had ever seen. Sometimes when the tide was out, we could walk out half a mile and see the tropical fish with their eloquent colors in the tide pools. In Genesis 1:31 it says, "And God saw everything He had made and, behold, it was very good." I agree with God; everything that God has made and that my eyes have seen is very good.

In fall of that year, the war was over and I was heading home. I was discharged in the spring of 1946, and I thought that the world was my oyster. Everybody, look out! I was soon to learn another lesson in life: that one doesn't live one's life alone.

After the War

I was invited to go out to Idaho with my brother, and I ended up owning an interest in a dairy. This was a twenty-four-hour-a-day job. We would milk the cows, bottle the milk, deliver the milk, and collect payment. Things were pretty hectic for this young guy. Since I had not graduated from high school, I thought that I should do that.

While at high school, I saw this red-haired beauty who was later to become the joy of my life. When she said that she would marry me, I thought, *Now the world is* really *my oyster*. We were married in 1947, and in the spring of 1948 we moved back to South Dakota where I became a farmer. The years of learning continued.

CHAPTER 2

Searching

Ask, and you will receive; seek, and you will find;
knock, and the door will be opened to you. (Matt. 7:7)

November 2, 1953, was a cold and dismal day, and it seemed that winter had come too soon ... again. Gaggles of Canada geese had long since flown over, heading for their warm wintering grounds in Texas. It seemed like it was an unusually cold day as I rolled out of bed and then hurried through the morning chores, milking the cows, feeding the chickens, etc. I was rushing because of a call I received the day before. The local feed store owner wanted me to drive into Nebraska to pick up a load of cattle feed, later to be delivered to a rancher.

We were poor but hadn't missed any meals, so whenever any extra work was available, I took it. Some would say that we, like many others, were living hand-to-mouth during those times. There were things going on in my life that I didn't fully understand, but looking back on it now, I see that God was dealing with the large void in my life. I had known then that something was missing.

I remember the Sunday before, when my wife, Donna, and I were sitting at the kitchen table for breakfast. We were talking about some things pertaining to God—spiritual things. I don't remember how this conversation got started, but it was the beginning of God's intervention in my life, eventually leading me to the cross of Christ for salvation. As I crushed out a cigarette, I said to Donna, "You know, I think I'll be a Christian, whether God does anything for me or not." I was so ignorant of what God had in mind for me.

I decided we should go to church, and so we got ready and drove the twenty-five miles to a church. We weren't there long when the offering plate was passed. Ordinarily that would have made me angry, but I thought, *If I'm going for this Christian stuff, I'd better put something in.* Well, I only had a ten dollar bill, so I threw it in. When the sermon started, my discomfort level rose, leading me to ask myself, *What are we doing here?* The preacher was an old fellow, and it seemed to me that he did more crying and laughing than talking. It seemed as though all the other people thought he was doing all right. We left the service as empty as we came.

Back to my all-day trucking job: I wouldn't get to my destination to pick up the cattle feed until noon. With that heavy load, it would be a long, slow drag home, because the trucks back then didn't have the power for climbing hills. Most of the time it would be pretty dark by the time I made it home. As a rule, though, I really enjoyed going on this little trip. I always liked to see the wildlife that would be out early in the mornings and evenings. I'd see foxes and coyotes in South Dakota, and then, as I would go up through the pines in northern Nebraska, I'd see wild turkeys and deer.

This morning as I started my journey, it seemed like it was so dark … a dark, dark day that seemed to settle down on me—I mean, right into my soul. Was this all there was to life? Surely there must be something more. What was the point of my existence? We had lost a little boy child in June. He lived fewer than thirty hours. As we laid this child in the grave, I experienced some serious grief. The worst of it was that I thought it must have been my fault that we lost this child. If only I could have "gotten a grip" on myself and lived a better life, then maybe God would have spared our son. God had given us four children, and all of them were miracle babies, as I will explain. How could anyone look at one of these little ones and not believe that?

God gave us Larry first, and then, four years later, we were blessed with Michael. He was a very healthy boy, full of life, and he seemed to be so happy. He was so easy to love. A year later, little Wayne tried to make his appearance into this world after seven months, but he couldn't survive beyond a few hours after birth. Even though he didn't live, the Lord certainly used Wayne's coming and going to make an impact on my life. Three years later, along came our only daughter, Elaine. Our family was complete. What a joy it was to have a little girl in our home.

From the start, it seemed like God had chosen our oldest son, Larry, to go through some things that most people would never have to face. Larry was exposed to whooping cough at seven months of age. The doctor told us that whooping cough killed 95 percent of babies that young who had contracted it. We had taken Larry to the doctor to see if we could get a shot to ease it a little; maybe we could pull him through. That was the day that we were to get the shock of our lives. After the examination, the doctor called us in and told us that Larry was a blue baby. The news was so heavy for Donna to bear; she wept but still had the strength to pull me through this horrible time. In other words, Larry was born with a heart defect and, without an outright miracle or surgery, he would most certainly have a very short life. It got to the point that Larry would lie around on the couch with no energy because his heart couldn't seem to do the work that it was meant to do.

When Larry was about three, we were told that we had better take him to Denver to the heart specialist and see what could be done. There was this little born-again Christian lady, Alta, who lived on the next farm down the road. As God would have it, she befriended us a number of times, so when she learned about our trip to Denver with Larry, she asked if she could ride along to see her son who lived there. It would have been really hard for us to say no.

Alta managed to be with us when Larry was undergoing the medical tests he needed to have. As we sat in the waiting room with nothing to do, this little lady began to talk about the things of God, which I didn't want to hear. I would have liked it better if we could have been talking about something else … anything. She shared with me the fact that a Christian could know he was saved and made ready for heaven. I had never really heard that, or at least I never understood it. But as my mind began to mull this over, I thought, *Yes, that is what everybody would want to know.* You'd be crazy not to want to know that, if it was possible. I believe that I became a seeker of the truth at that very moment.

Well, the doctor finally finished the tests and came out to tell us the news. He said that Larry would have to have an operation to survive. My heart was overwhelmed with grief as I thought, *Oh no, God is going to take another one of our children.* I told my wife, "Let's get out of here," as though we could run from this horrific thing that we would have to deal with eventually.

We hadn't been home long when I remembered what Alta had said. "The Bible plainly tells us that we can know beyond a shadow of doubt that we are saved and ready for heaven." Now, my wife comes from a background where the Bible was never discussed. Somehow I really didn't want her to know that I was serious about seeking the Lord … yet the seed that had been planted was starting to grow, and I wanted to find the Scripture that said that I could know. I found an old Bible, and I would go upstairs by myself and try to find the passage. Due to my complete ignorance of the Scripture, however, I couldn't find it.

Because of something that took place in the church of my youth, I came to the conclusion that all preachers were nuts and that anybody who went to church was probably crazy, too. The world was so full of hypocrisy, and I knew I didn't want to be a hypocrite. My brother-in-law had a big dance hall, and one night I helped him to mark the people as they came in. It seemed to me that so many of them would say, "Put the mark in my palm, because I'm going to church in the morning and I don't want anyone to see that I'd been here." I felt disgusted by this type of behavior, and I thought the best thing for me was to stay as far away from that type of person as I could. So far, I had been pretty successful, except for Alta, who had gotten deeper into my soul than I wanted to admit. It always amazes me how God slipped that little lady into my life and how what she had said was having a much larger effect on me than I'd ever admit. So how can I decide if this Christianity is something I want to be involved with? Alta is certainly genuine but what about those guys at the dance hall? One thing that we need to remember: in order for there to be a counterfeit Christian, there has to be the real, genuine thing.

There was a battle going on in my life. One minute I'd wanted to find the truth, and then the next minute I didn't want anything to do with it. My search continued, but again, due to my ignorance of the Scriptures, I couldn't find the knowledge I sought.

I thought back to when I was probably eight or ten, when a big tent was set up in town and it was announced that there was going to be a revival meeting. It almost seemed like it should have been a circus. It was summertime and, because of the heat, the men would roll up the sides of the tent to make it more comfortable for the people inside. The preachers all dressed alike in black suits and black ties with white shirts. Now, to this young boy, their voices sounded about as near to God's voice as I would ever hear on this earth. It did seem like the Lord gave them loud, clear voices as they pronounced the doom of the unbeliever. They were so loud that people said they could be heard all over town. Anyway, the reason I thought this event was somewhat like a circus is because about 15 percent of the people from the surrounding farming area were on the inside of the tent, and the other 85 percent were on the outside. It was like the people on the inside were in the circus ring performing for the crowd that was on the outside. I guess the ones on the outside, probably from seventy-five to a hundred and fifty people, thought they were really having fun. At night they would sit just outside, in the light coming from the tent, and hoot and holler and make fun of the preacher. Also, during the altar call, they would cry out names of people in the tent and taunt them. For them it seemed like a time of real jubilee. Sometimes for a little more fun they would slip in and cut the tent ropes so the tent would start to collapse. Of course, the men inside jumped to the rescue to prevent the tent from collapsing. After the first time the hecklers cut the ropes, the people inside the tent designated a guard to stand watch on the outside to prevent a recurrence. Even at my young age, I realized that Christians receive reproach or scorn for their faith. I knew those people who were outside the tent were making fun of what I thought must be God's business.

I look back at what happened to some of those people. I'm sure that if they had it to do over again, they would choose to be inside the tent rather than outside with the scoffers. We do have a choice. It must have been a tearful occasion when the people stood around Noah's ark as it commenced to rain. Imagine with me for a moment how the howling and mockery they were throwing at Noah and his family started quieting down. They had thought they were having fun. But now their shouts were turning from jubilee to cries and tears, but the day of grace had passed for them. God closed the door of the ark. It was judgment day for that crowd forever.

My little-boy heart certainly heard and understood enough of the gospel that was preached that day to know that I was guilty and deserved to go to hell. The only thing that I didn't comprehend was that *through grace I could be saved.* Those preachers bore down heavy with the assertion that we should make restitution for all the wrong we had done to others, and they also insisted that we should repent. I remember that I even went to a few people and tried to make peace for the wrong that I had done to them. Finally, after a month or so, the tent was taken down, and with it went my chance to ever really get right with God. It seemed like there was no hope for this soul. Praise God, there was more to come.

CHAPTER 3

River of Living Water

Whoever believes in me, as Scripture has said,
rivers of living water will flow from within them.
(John 7:38 NIV)

My journey continued after I delivered the load of cattle feed. That November day, the low, dark, cold clouds were rolling in with a promise that winter would soon be here. It was almost like a foreboding of dark, desperate days ahead of me, without hope of anything getting better. My soul in despair commenced to talk to God, not really knowing for sure that He was listening, but I *really* wanted to know if He was.

Satan had planted a seed in my heart that told me that I would have to work and do some great thing to even up the score for what Jesus had done for me on the cross of Calvary. I didn't know that I could never do enough to "win" salvation. I didn't understand then what Romans 3 says: "Therefore no one will be declared righteous in God's sight by the works of the law."

At the time, I was a two-pack-a-day cigarette smoker and always felt it was wrong for me, yet it was a dilemma because, try as I might, I couldn't quit the habit that had taken such a strong hold of me. The Scripture says not to defile your body because it is the temple of the Holy Ghost.

I was experiencing a deep godly sorrow, with repentance in my heart for all the wrong that I had ever done. Through the darkness of that godly sorrow came these words from heaven: "Only believe, Bruce, that Jesus died for the forgiveness and remission of all your sins." As that entered my mind, God filled my heart with faith, and I believed. Praise God! I have found it! I have found it! The pearl of great price. For the first time, I knew that I was now a child of God, washed in that precious blood of His dear son; I was born again and I was free, free … *free*. I can only attempt to tell you what really happened. I fell in love with Jesus Christ, the Lord of heaven and earth, that day, and that love is still the same today, all these years later. I believe that God gave me nothing less than a heart transplant. He took that old heart of self-righteousness and replaced it with one that was totally submitted to Him, one full and running over with love for Him and everybody else. O how that heavy load of sin was gone, the one that Satan had strapped onto my back and that I carried for twenty-seven years. Alleluia!

These words from an old hymn, "O now I see the cleansing wave", ran through my mind.

> I rise to walk in heaven's own land,
> Above the world and sin …
> And Jesus, only Jesus, knows,
> My Jesus crucified …
> The cleansing stream I see, I see,
> I plunge, and O, it cleanseth me,
> It cleanseth me, yes, cleanseth me

I believe that God in His love literally opened a window in heaven and let some of His glory pour out of it and into my unworthy soul. O the peace of God that passeth all understanding, the joy unspeakable and full of glory, was all mine. The precious words from another hymn "O the love that drew salvation's plan" came to mind.

O the love that drew salvation's plan,
O the grace that brought it down to man.

The love of God that entered into my heart at this time was so great that I noticed right away when I heard someone use God's name in vain. It literally hurt my inner being. That dark day had turned into the best day of my life. O to think that Jesus would lay down His life for such a one as I. All those years, Satan had me deceived into thinking that somehow I had to make myself a better person. I had to lift myself up out of the miry clay before I could be accepted by God. How could anyone pull himself up by his own bootstraps and into heaven?

I had heard my little boy following in my footsteps, using God's name in vain, and I thought I had better cut that out. But it wasn't in me to stop using profanity any more than it was in me to stop smoking. Yet, when Jesus came into my life that day, all those things that were not pleasing to God had to go out the window, and so they did: cigarettes, swearing, and a lot more. There were only a couple times when the craving for cigarettes came back. When this happened, I'd call on Jesus, and it was gone. Praise God forever, I was free from that filthy habit. I didn't at the time realize just how much the Lord had done for me.

A couple of weeks later, I was hammering on a nail and I hit my finger. It hurt so bad that curses would normally be coming out of my mouth in long ugly strings. It was then that I realized there wasn't a swearword in my mind. As I looked at that hurting finger, I was literally overcome with gratitude to my newfound friend Jesus for delivering me from swearing. Best of all, that was years ago, and those swearwords are still gone. I had been made a new creature in Christ.

> Therefore, if anyone is in Christ, the new creation has come: The old has gone, the new is here! (2 Cor. 5:17)

If you can believe, you are blessed, as Jesus told Thomas.

> Then Jesus told him, "Because you have seen me, you have believed; blessed are those who have not seen and yet have believed." (John 20:29)

I would like to mention at this time the rivers of living water that John talks about. As Jesus came into my life that day, this river of living water started to flow.

> Whoever believes in me, as Scripture has said, rivers of living water will flow from within them." By this he meant the Spirit, whom those who believed in him were later to receive. Up to that time the Spirit had not been given, since Jesus had not yet been glorified. (John 7:38–39)

Can you see? Jesus has been glorified. This river is available now to every believer. To me, this river of living water is the most precious thing that a Christian has to witness to his or her own soul. What a miracle that the Holy Ghost literally dwells within your heart. I want to try and explain just what this is, so as not to confuse anyone. This river started flowing the moment that I first believed in Jesus. It makes me weep and laugh at the same time, and it overflows in my heart so that it feels it might burst with praise, thanksgiving, joy, gratitude, love, and complete worship of Jesus, who loved me so much that He laid down His precious life for one such as I.

Christ had forgiven me of so much. Paul explained it best when he said that he was the chief of sinners. I believe that description certainly applied to me. It will surely build your confidence when you begin to comprehend that He has taken your sins away, never to remember them again, as the following Scripture states.

> As far as the east is from the west, so far has he removed our transgressions from us. (Ps. 103:12)

Think about what He said in this Scripture, that the east will never meet the west, and that the west will never meet the east. This knowledge should be enough to start a river of joy flowing into your heart.

When I was in business, we would have to develop springs of water. I'd like to make a comparison here, as the idea parallels the concept of the river of living water that Jesus speaks about. Many times there would be seepage of water coming up from the ground, so we would go in with a backhoe and begin to take out dirt and dig deeper, removing any rubble or anything that might fall in. As we took out the debris, the water would begin to run more and more, until finally there would be a stream big enough to water the cattle, the household, the town, or whatever there was that needed a drink. Such is also the way with this spring of living water that the Lord gives us. We can allow Satan to come in and start polluting our spring to the point where it slows down and almost stops, leaving only a wet spot on the ground. We need to be wise to Satan and, with God's help, throw a hedge around that spring so he can't get in and pollute it. Old Satan is smart enough to know that we wouldn't let him come in and clog it all at once, so he starts out slow and easy. Old Satan knows that Jesus said to abstain from the very appearance of evil. There is no need for me to mention any certain thing, because the Holy Spirit that dwells within will warn you. We need to obey Him, for He is able to keep that which we have committed unto Him, as Luke 21:34 says, "And take heed to yourselves, lest at any time your hearts be overcharged with surfeiting, and drunkenness, and cares of this life, and so that day come upon you unawares."

This water that I'm talking about will not only quench your thirst and provide the spiritual nourishment that we all need, but it will also cleanse your mind of the darkness and sin that Satan loads his people with. That's why the children of the Lord are so happy and free. God wants us to carefully guard our spring of living water and share it with the world around us. Others are thirsty also. The Bible says, "And let him that is athirst come. And whosoever will, let him take the water of life freely" (Rev. 22:17).

Many things will stop the flow of water: if you quit reading God's Word, quit praying, quit witnessing to others, quit going to church—the water will stop. These things really are fatal to that precious flow that we need. We won't always be overjoyed by the wonderful feeling that this spring of living water sometimes brings. Many times we will allow things into our life that will stop it. At these times, however, the Lord might just chasten us:

> Now no chastening seems to be joyful for the present, but painful; nevertheless, afterward it yields the peaceable fruit of righteousness to those who have been trained by it. (Heb. 12:11 NKJV)

When we are going through the valleys and being chastened by the Lord, it can get pretty dark. The Lord has already been through everything that could possibly come our way, so when we are in a tough spot, that is the time to trust Him. He will take us through to that hilltop over there, and we will see that the sun is still shining. The first trial or test that the Lord will allow us to go through will seem so hard, but as we grow and He continues to lead us through more and more difficult places, we will look back on the first trial and think, *Why did I think that was so hard?*

When we are first saved, we are like a newborn baby. All we know how to do is cry, eat, and make a mess. We need to do what Timothy says in the following Scripture.

> Study to shew thyself approved unto God, a workman that needeth not to be ashamed, rightly dividing the word of truth. (2 Tim. 2:15)

If we do this, we will see ourselves growing up in the Lord, and we will experience in a new way that river gently flowing as we let Jesus lead us along.

When I got home that November night after I first came to believe in Jesus, I went into the house and told my wife that the Lord had saved me. I was so filled with the fullness of God that, like I said before, I was crying and laughing and praising God all at the same time. I don't know just what Donna thought, other than that for sure something had happened to her husband. For some reason that only God knows, that little Christian neighbor lady, Alta, who had always bugged me, or so I thought, just happened to drop by just then, and of course we had a time of rejoicing. The Bible says that the angels in heaven rejoice over one sinner who has been redeemed. Alta went to be with the Lord a number of years ago. I'm so thankful today for the part she played in my search for the truth. I love her dearly.

The Bible came alive to my soul; I read it every chance I had. I remember several weeks after the Lord had come into my life, I got to thinking that there must be something wrong with me. Nobody should feel as good every day and be so happy. I was a newborn babe in Christ and had so much to learn. I finally came to Romans 8:1, and then I understood that there was no mistake; I could go ahead and be happy. It says, "There is therefore now no condemnation to them that are in Christ Jesus, who walk not after the flesh, but after the spirit. For 'the law of the Spirit of life in Christ Jesus' hath made me free from the law of sin and death."

There is an old song, "Glory to God Hallelujah", that says,

> Yes, the children of the Lord
> have a right to shout and sing …
> Glory to God! Alleluia!

I didn't have to carry that heavy load of condemnation and guilt for my sin anymore. No wonder a new Christian has the feeling that he is almost flying. Jesus took that load off my back forever.

At the time, I wondered how Donna would come to share my newfound faith.

CHAPTER 4

Growing in Faith and Sanctification

The winter seemed to pass so quickly with my newfound companion, my Lord, Savior, and friend. It was like an old song says, "The sky is bluer, the grass is greener," and in this case the snow was whiter. Seeing new snow fall was a reminder that Jesus had washed away my sins and made me whiter than snow.

My wife, Donna, had come from a background of complete biblical darkness, so when I arrived home that night with the glory of God on my face, it was puzzling to her. She could see that I was a new man; there had been quite a change. Here was a man full of love for Christ and the desire to know Him more deeply. She knew how I'd failed at attempts to quit smoking and swearing. There was no denying what had happened. I wanted to just grab her and pull her into "the kingdom," but I soon found out that I couldn't do that. I would give her Scripture and pray that God would help her to see what Jesus wanted to do for her. Well, nearly two months had passed, and disharmony was developing in our household. Just that afternoon she told me she didn't want anything to do with my religion and to leave her alone. Needless to say, this put a real burden on my heart, because I knew that if God didn't do a work in her heart, then our marriage would be rocky.

It was Sunday, January 1, and I was earnestly praying as I was doing the evening chores. I remember telling God that I couldn't bring

Donna to salvation and that He would have to take over. I didn't think that she would be going to church with me that evening, but she did actually go. She had an appointment with Jesus, it seemed. That night, on January 1, Donna knelt down before God and committed her life to the Lord. Our home was now more in harmony than it had been before because of our shared love of God. The Lord used the Christian neighbor lady I've mentioned before, to lead Donna to a relationship with Christ. As we look back on it now, we see God's plan unfolding in such a precious and powerful way. Never discount the power of prayer and testimony.

The Hunting License

I'll interject a short story that illustrates how God had been working on my sinful nature. Shortly after I came to the Lord but before Donna had, it seemed as if He tapped me on the shoulder a number of times about things that I had done, reminding me that He wanted me to clean things up. I said that I wanted to make restitution and would do it as fast as I could. He told me that He would help. One such incident took place one night as I was milking the cows. He reminded me of an elk hunting trip to Idaho. He said, "Remember that time you went elk hunting on a resident license but should have paid for a more costly nonresident license?" I remembered it, all right. Whether it was my pride or Satan, I really don't know, but I came up with a lot of arguments against why I should have to make it right. One of them was that my wife hadn't been convicted yet, and if I confessed, the authorities would make an example of me and throw the book at me, take my rifle, or even throw me in jail. If that happened, Donna might never know Jesus. This was really a hard one for me; would I obey the Lord at any cost, or would my old nature have its way? I thank God that Jesus won out. I wrote a letter to the Idaho Department of Fish and Game confessing my wrong, telling them why I was writing, mentioning my newfound friend, and saying that I wanted to make things right. When I mailed that letter, I knew truth had won out, and I was at complete peace with a clean conscience. A couple of weeks went by before I got an official response saying that the Idaho Department of Fish and Game was not in a place to make a moral judgment, but they were sorry that I had to hunt under such unpleasant circumstances. The letter went on to say that there would be no penalty, and they hoped that I would come and hunt there again. So the argument that my pride (or Satan) made would have cheated me out of a blessing. The Lord knows what is ahead, and I believe He was just preparing me for what was to come—using any way to keep that river of living water flowing at its best, as the song says.

> Trust and obey, for there is no other way
> To be happy in Jesus, than to trust and obey.

As newborn babes in Christ, my wife and I commenced praying that God would save my wife's parents who were wheat farmers and pretty much left God out of their lives. They had done well financially and, as is the case with so many people seemingly doing well in their lives, didn't see a need to change. We were truly burdened for them and prayed in earnest that they might be convicted and come to the Lord. As far as we know, they never accepted Jesus as their personal Savior. We can only hope that sometime before their deaths they had made a commitment.

CHAPTER 5

The Love of God

It was the spring of 1955; my folks had made a trip from Washington State to be with us. It was such a joy to have them. At that time, Donna and I had personally known God for just over a year. We had so much more to talk about now. My folks had been Christians for at least twenty years, but since I really didn't speak the same language as they did until I was reborn, many times we didn't have much to talk about. So now, being on the same wavelength, we were having a great time. This particular morning, as we went about the morning chores, Dad and I were talking about how great it was to be a Christian and were just enjoying some wonderful fellowship together. I experienced such a radical change in my life that I was just as excited this day as I was on the day Jesus came into my life.

I remember telling Dad that this love of God was so precious to me that I would rather lose everything that we had accumulated than lose the love of God out of my heart. I was still what you would call a "babe in Christ," but every day Jesus seemed to grow more precious.

Later on in the day, we decided that we had to go uptown, twenty-five miles away, to do some business. Little did we know what awaited us. When we have Jesus as our pilot, we don't have to know the future, because we know who holds the future in His hands. If trouble comes, we can say with David in Psalm 121, lines 2, 7, and 8:

"My help cometh from the Lord, which made heaven and earth. ... The Lord shall preserve thee from all evil: He shall preserve thy soul. ... The Lord shall preserve thy going out and thy coming in from this time forth, and even forever more."

This is exactly what the Lord did, as you will see. Donna and I had purchased a nearly new GMC truck with really low mileage. Because we had the funds and we came across this deal, we believed that the Lord had given it to us. We were so thankful, knowing that it would surely be used to good advantage on the farm. It was exactly what we needed, and I figured it would last us a good number of years. As with many farm vehicles, the truck was registered but uninsured. It wasn't the law at that time to have insurance on the truck. Down on the farm, the truck was mostly used off the road. In those days, we didn't insure a lot of things, sometimes because of lack of money, but also because I felt like the Lord would see us through.

About a week before this incident I am about to describe, I loaned this truck to a childhood friend. This friend had committed his life to the Lord and was in the ministry. He wanted to borrow our truck to move his furniture to Arizona, as I recall. Without question, I loaned it to him. After all, a brother was in need. We felt that everything we had belonged to the Lord, and whoever needed it should have it.

> Give to the one who asks you, and do not turn away from
> the one who wants to borrow from you. (Matt. 5:42)

As my dad and I were going to town and coming down the road to the Cheyenne River Bridge, we could see a car and truck wreck. I wondered, *Are my eyes deceiving me, or is that our truck?* The truck, our truck, was sitting on our side of the bridge with the frame bent around at a crazy angle. On the other side of the bridge was a new but smashed car that had been towed after the crash. We recognized the car as belonging to Jack, a neighbor. Later it was determined that both vehicles were totaled. My heart sank as I remembered that we didn't have insurance on the truck, and I was immediately reminded of what I had told Dad: that I'd rather lose everything than lose the love of God from my heart. What irony! Was God testing me as He did with Peter after Peter said that he would never deny Jesus?

> And Peter remembered the word of Jesus, which said unto him, Before the cock crow, thou shalt deny me thrice. And he went out, and wept bitterly. (Matt. 26:75)

We were not there to see the accident, but this is what apparently happened. Our truck, driven by my friend, was coming down a steep road with a washboard surface. The truck began to bounce so much that as the truck approached the bridge, my friend lost control. Jack's car was coming off the bridge and had nowhere to go, so he collided with my truck. A highway patrolman was still at the scene, so we asked if anyone was hurt. He said it looked really bad and the car passengers had been taken to the hospital, but as far as he knew they were all alive.

There was quite a long hill to climb as we left the bridge and headed toward town. My dad was in the backseat, and I remember that as we started up that hill, he commenced to pray out loud. If I live for a thousand years I will never be able to tell you how grateful I am for having Christian parents. It was like reinforcement dropped right out of heaven. Before I was up the hill, the Lord spoke to my heart and gave me this well-known Romans 8:28 Scripture to dwell on. "And we know that all things work together for good to them that love God, to them who are the called according to His purpose." What assurance straight from heaven! Yes, the peace that came over me was real.

I felt like I had been cuddled under the wings of the almighty God of my salvation. What a wonderful place to be at a time like this. Without God in our lives, my dad and I would have been worried sick. At the hospital, we were pleasantly surprised to find that no one was badly hurt. Many small cuts made a bloody crash scene, so I certainly understood why the patrolman came to the conclusion that he did.

Now was the time when we got right down to where the rubber meets the road. How am I going to pay Jack for his car that was damaged by my truck, for the hospital bills, and for the clothes, now bloodstained, ruined in the crash? Once again I remembered what I had told Dad that morning, how I would rather lose everything than lose the love of God from my heart. I also recalled the Word of God that came to my heart that morning: "All things work together for good to them that love God ..."

A few days later I was able to get in touch with my friend who had borrowed the truck, and so I talked to him. What great news it was that because he had bought a new car that year on a payment plan he was required to purchase car insurance. Because my friend borrowed the truck and I had not charged him for its use, his insurance covered the car, all medical bills, the clothes, and everything except my truck. *All glory be to God!*

One sometimes wonders why things like this happen. Could it be that others might be brought to faith? One day as I was working on some machinery, Jack came visiting. He had previously signed a release of my liability, but somehow I knew that he wanted more. Sure enough, he let it be known that he didn't think he had gotten enough out of the insurance company. He was quick to mention that he had a field of oats that he thought I should combine for him for free. Although it was not logical that I should be supplementing Jack's insurance company's payment, I had no problem agreeing to his request. I had been praying for him and his wife ever since the wreck. So when he joined me on the combine, I was able to share Jesus with him. I told him that Jesus was available to him, too. The seed was planted (Luke 8: "The seed is God's Word"). I don't know what kind of soil that seed fell on, but I will be so happy to see Jack in glory.

I'm writing these things so that you might know that if you make a full and complete commitment to God, you will never come out the loser. I may have lost a good truck in this deal, but the Lord has given me a number of trucks since that day, every one better than the one I lost. Even if He hadn't, I feel like I've been more than well paid by how He took care of me and brought me out of an impossible situation.

The next spring, we would go through the first miracle having to do with our son and our parents' first grandson, Larry.

CHAPTER 6

"You Saw a Miracle"

Verily, verily, I say unto you, He that believeth on me, the works that I do shall he do also; and greater works than these shall he do; because I go unto my Father. (John 14:12)

It was the first part of June, a beautiful time of the year. Spring had sprung. We lived right next to a dry creek except for the spring runoff. Sometimes the creek would run for a month. It was full and running at this time. The birds had all migrated back by this time and were competing for nest sites, so the air was full of their songs. It seemed as though they would burst their little hearts out trying to be heard.

This particular morning, my wife, Donna, and her mother had gone to town about thirty-five miles away to get groceries and do some shopping. That left my father-in-law, my five-year-old son Larry, and me at home. We had this big old barn that the years and weather had ravaged; it didn't have a lot of time left before it fell down. We were busy taking it down and salvaging the lumber to build a smaller barn. Times were changing so fast. We had no use for the big barns anymore. We used to need the barn for the horses that did the farmwork there in South Dakota. When I was a child we needed it since we milked a bunch of cows, and in the winter it was nice to get in from the snowstorms to milk the warm cows. I remember storms in the 1950s when the snow would pile up so high and be packed so hard that the cows could walk on it and over the fences.

My father-in-law and I had torn off a bunch of worn-out shingles from the barn roof and were planning to burn them down by the creek. We were there by the creek pushing the shingles out of the truck, and I guess we got so busy that we weren't watching what Larry was doing. We were about to light the shingles on fire when we noticed that Larry was missing. Kids like to get a campfire burning, and Larry would be right in on this if he could. We were about an eighth of a mile from the house, so I let out a holler for Larry to come see the fire, but there was no answer. My father-in-law walked over by the creek, forty feet away, and there under a box elder tree that had grown out over the water was Larry's hat, circling in a whirlpool.

Crawling Out on a Limb, Larry Fell into the Water

Photo courtesy of Jenalyn Ferguson, a.k.a. Jag Fergus

The creek was in flood stage and the water was really dirty brown because the creek hadn't run long enough to get clear. When I saw

Larry's hat, I knew that he was in the water. In complete desperation I dove in, knowing that my son was in there and that I had to find him. The miracle of this story started right then. It could have taken hours to find Larry, but I knew I had to find him *now*. I remember how cold that water was when I dove in. Miraculously, my foot hit something during that frigid plunge. Praise the Lord, it was Larry. I grabbed my boy and came up out of the water in a panic. His little face had turned blue. I can't describe how helpless and desperate I felt. Only God knew how long he had been in the water. I could see no signs of life. God was the only one who could help him now. I was literally screaming at the top of my voice to the Lord, asking Him to let us have Larry back. I laid Larry on the ground, facedown. Other than cry out to almighty God, I didn't know what to do, since I never had any training for an emergency like this. I had to believe that the Lord had me doing the right thing.

My father-in-law was going through pure agony. This was his first grandchild, and now he was gone. I can still see him wringing his hands in grief. I don't know how much time went by before Larry made a noise and we knew that God was there and had saved my son. I'll never forget when my father-in-law heard him grunt. He literally shouted, "He's alive ... he's alive!" I can't begin to describe the gratitude and praise to God that welled up in my heart for God's demonstration of His love for and mercy toward us that day. As great a miracle as this was to us, it was made all the sweeter when Larry's heart condition was finally fixed at age nine. Even my father-in-law later confessed that, "What I saw was beyond anything one could explain ... The richness in knowing God was beyond what money could buy."

Larry was born with a damaged heart and diagnosed as a blue baby. As time went on, his condition worsened. When he was nine, we knew that we would have to get help for Larry or else he would not live much longer. Needless to say, we had been in prayer many times concerning his condition.

The Fleece
(A Test of God's Will as Recorded in Judges 6)

We were poor farmers, and our farm income would have to get much stronger before we could afford an operation for Larry. The reality of our situation was that our financial health was only as good as the last harvest and the price of the grain. If Larry was to have an operation, we needed a sign. I was led by the Lord to "put out a fleece." It was really quite simple. Our farm was on dry land, and at that time we never fertilized. That year we had several hundred acres of winter wheat. It had rained a lot, and the wheat was going to yield well (it actually yielded about sixty bushels per acre). The fleece was that the Lord would have me harvest it all myself with my own little fourteen-foot combine, resulting in a harvest that could pay for Larry's operation. The history of farming in South Dakota wouldn't indicate that I had much of a chance to succeed. The wind was violent at times, and a number of times it destroyed the whole crop ... like a couple of years before when a storm destroyed our wheat crop just before harvest. The hail beat the stocks into the ground so badly that you couldn't tell that one swath had already been cut through the field. This fleece was for real. A bad crop meant no operation, and a good crop meant help for our fading son Larry.

The wheat ripened and we began to harvest. What a harvest! Never before or since have we enjoyed such a bountiful crop. The wheat was so ripe that the husks had opened up and it seemed like the kernels of wheat were just hanging there. A windstorm now would be a disaster. It was Saturday afternoon; we had two eighty-acre fields left to harvest. The custom combiners (farmers coming north to harvest other crops after having done their own) had pretty well finished the harvest in the area and were ready to move on. One of them saw our fields that weren't harvested and had stopped to see if he could get the job. Needless to say, by this time my nerves were wearing thin and I thought it sure would be nice to have that wheat in a bin away from the hail danger. So in my weakness I told him he could cut it, but he would have to wait until Monday because we were Christians and always shut down fieldwork on Sundays. God had done so much for us that we wanted to honor Him on His day. This made the guy mad, so down the road he went.

What a miracle it was for the wheat to stay in the heads until we got down to the last twenty acres, which is when the combine finally broke down. I believe that if I hadn't asked for the combiners' help, I would have finished the whole job myself. But I took it into my own hands and hired a couple of combiners to finish the harvest. That wasn't the original deal I had with God, and so, you guessed it, we lost some wheat. He is the Master of the wind, and He certainly stopped it from damaging our crop. He is always faithful, and He expects us to be, too. I thank Him so much that even in our weakness He is faithful and forgives us, helping us to go on serving Him. I hoped that I had learned a lesson, never to doubt our Great Creator. When the harvest was in, there was no doubt or fear (financial- or outcome-wise) in our minds concerning the upcoming heart operation.

The Heart Surgery

We took Larry to Denver, and he had the first operation. After it was finished, the doctor came into the waiting room to tell us that the operation was a success and not to worry. He sat there a while visiting and telling us what he could about the operation, and then turned to me and asked, "Did anything ever happen to Larry?"

We didn't know what he had seen or why he was asking, but we responded, "Well, yes." Then I recounted the story of his drowning at age five.

When I had finished, the doctor just shook his head and thoughtfully replied, "You saw a miracle." Given the condition of Larry's heart, the doctor realized that there was no way that weakened heart could have started again.

I said, "Praise the Lord, Doc!" I knew all the time it was a miracle, but I was glad to hear him say it. Now others would know and believe how great God is and know that He can be reached in times of trouble. *Praise His holy name, and all glory be to God.*

Many times I slip into thinking that a particular burden, whatever it might be, is all on my shoulders and that it's just too heavy to bear. I tend to get discouraged. But Jesus said, "Come unto me, all ye that labour and are heavy laden, and I will give you rest. Take my yoke upon you, and learn of me; for I am meek and lowly in heart: and ye shall find rest unto your souls. For my yoke is easy, and my burden is light" (Matt. 11:28–30).

Larry's operation—called pure pulmonary stenosis—seemed to be a real success. It was as though all his life he had been tied up, but now the ropes had been cut and he was free. It was within the week that he and another little boy who had had the same operation were out of bed and playing with Hula-Hoops. It was so soon that it somewhat alarmed us, but the doctor said it was okay.

Let me add a story about an incident that normally would have caused a fuss but which, at such a time of rejoicing, only resulted in a smile. We left Denver with happy and thankful hearts. It was such a pleasure to see Larry more alive than he had seemed for a long time. We had left our other children there on the farm with Grandma Gail. Our German shepherd watchdog, Sheba, was there to protect the family and Grandma Gail. Although Sheba was a pushover as a watchdog, her size would make anyone back off. Anyway, this dear lady had set out a five-gallon bucket of drinking water for Sheba. As we got home, parked the car, and came around to the door, to our amusement and dismay there was our little daughter (not quite two) using her shoe for a cup to get a drink out of Sheba's water bucket. Who could be stern at such a time? All we could do was thank the Lord for guardian angels. Years later, our daughter is still healthy. I guess there was no damage done.

Later in his adult life, Larry had another operation to repair a hole between the chambers of his heart. He is currently leading a near normal life in Seattle, Washington. He has two grown children and he loves the Lord. For all these things, we are very thankful.

The Lord Jesus Christ saw us through all of the hard places and times of complete despair, and I just want to give Him all glory and honor. I would hate to have to face life without Him. However, Larry's was not to be the only life-and-death situation my family had to deal with. Years later I found myself buried alive.

Backhoe

Laying Pipe in the Country

Burying Pipe

CHAPTER 7

Buried Alive

Our family had been in the pipeline business for nearly a dozen years and had installed many miles of pipeline in the countryside. In South Dakota, the cattle pastures are big, and the only source of water for the cattle in the dry season is an occasional dam or else dugouts that catch rainwater and the runoff from melting snow. Some years it would be so dry by the middle of summer that the ponds below the dams would go dry or get so low and muddy that the water wasn't fit for the cattle to drink. The ranchers formed a co-op that funded the connection to an artesian well water supply and the miles of pipeline that were needed.

We had just been awarded a contract to install seventy-five hundred feet of water main in our little town. We started this job not realizing what the day had in store for us. This day, July 20, 1976, was Donna's and my twenty-ninth wedding anniversary; that evening, we were to celebrate the occasion. Still, at our ages we would be satisfied just to go out to dinner, relax, and contemplate just how good God had been to us.

We had been through what we thought were pretty rough times with our son Larry, given his heart problems, so we knew that life wasn't easy. Perhaps it isn't supposed to be easy. We were well aware of what God said in Hebrews:

> You have forgotten the encouragement that is
> addressed to you as sons: "My son, do not think
> lightly of the Lord's discipline or give up when you
> are corrected by him. For the Lord disciplines the
> one he loves, and he punishes every son he accepts."
> What you endure disciplines you: God is treating
> you as sons. Is there a son whom his father does not
> discipline? Now, if you are without any discipline, in
> which all sons share, then you are illegitimate and not
> God's sons. (Heb. 12:5-8 ISV)

We started the job with the threat of rain overhead—never a pleasant prospect when laying pipe. One of the first tasks had been to find the right pipe and the proper fittings for it, which would mean uncovering some of the existing pipe in order to identify the fittings needed for a proper hookup. We would seldom have all possible combinations of fittings in our shop that might be needed to avoid a fast sixty-mile trip to another town. This day it looked like rain, but we worried that we might waste the entire day if it didn't rain and we could be working, so we began the job anyway.

We found the existing pipe end without incident, we had the right fitting, and it looked like we were ready to continue with the job. The initial hookup was made, and one twenty-foot piece of pipe had been laid, when it began to rain. In bad weather there was always work we could do in the shop, working on other equipment and keeping things in good repair.

The day went fast as we did our backup jobs, and quitting time was approaching. Rather than leave the ditch open where we had begun to lay pipe, Mike, my youngest son, and I went back to fill in the ditch so it wouldn't be hazardous to the traffic during nighttime. I walked along the ditch as Mike was starting the backhoe. As I walked, I saw that a stone seemed to be lying against the newly laid pipe. The stone was unlikely to cause harm to the durable, bedded ductile pipe. Still, I decided to wrestle the rock to the side before Mike filled the thirty-by-six-by-four-foot ditch with the backhoe. I had no apprehension of danger whatsoever and felt completely safe walking with a shovel toward the end of the ditch to get out. Without warning, one of the rain-moistened ditch walls collapsed, knocking me over to the other side, pinning me against the standing wall, pulling me down, and covering my entire body with a foot and a half of heavy dirt and rock. In an instant I was buried alive.

I think death comes suddenly and without warning to a lot more people than you would think. Not many people plan for it. It just happens. When sudden calamity strikes, it's too late to make peace with God—or with anyone else, for that matter. God's Word says, "It is appointed unto man, once to die and after that the judgment" (Heb. 9:27).

How merciful our God is to warn us and give us a chance to repent and believe.

> Today if you will hear His voice, harden not your heart" (Heb. 4:7).

I felt I was already dead, with my body smashed and my life terminated. I thought how sad my wife would be, this happening on our wedding anniversary. There would be no celebration tonight … only tears. A deep sense of grief and regret came over me when I thought about all I was leaving behind: family, friends, the help I might have been able to render to others.

My mind was now in a strange place. Was it heaven, perhaps? I saw a book that closed before my eyes, and somehow I knew that it was my book. Sadness came over me as I thought I would never be able to help anyone or do anything for anyone ever again. I believe I was thinking about a passage in the Book of Revelation.

> And I saw the dead, small and great, stand before God; and the books were opened: and another book was opened, which is the book of life; and the dead were judged out of those things which were written in the book, according to their works. (Rev. 20:12)

At one time, nobody could believe that all the doings of people could be recorded in books … even in heaven. However, in this technical age of computers, it shouldn't be too hard to understand that God has a record of our lives. I certainly don't mean to downsize God to a mere computer, because Hebrews 4:12 says, "For the Word of God is quick, and powerful … and is a discerner of the thoughts and intents of the heart."

As Mike got into the backhoe to start it, he heard a thump. Looking around, he could see that the ditch wall had caved in, and he knew that I was in there somewhere. I can only imagine his anguish as he jumped into the ditch to see if he could hear or see anything— anything at all. But there were no clues, only rock and dirt. In his desperation, he moved a few rocks but could see that there was no way he could get me out in time by hand. This ditch was in an old roadway, so big rocks and hard dirt couldn't be removed by hand fast enough. This is where the miracle really began. Mike got into the backhoe, moved around next to the ditch, and began to dig, knowing full well that if he hit me with the bucket it would be devastating and might kill me. He also knew that he didn't have a choice. What a spot to be put in! It had to be the Lord's hand in the situation that kept him from panicking. All this time he was shouting, "Help!" as loud as he could to people who were likely at the fast-food restaurant next to the job site. Mike dug over my head twice, eight inches at a time versus the normal two or three feet. He was coming back the third time when the Lord told him to move over. He moved to the side and dug at least three more buckets out before the dirt rolled away from my head. If he hadn't seen my head and dug one more time, he would have killed me, but God was there to prevent that. Mike later told Donna, while he was sitting on the floor of the hospital with his back against a wall, "Mother, God was there."

I was hurt so badly that I couldn't maintain consciousness, but I remember hearing something from time to time. When I was in the ditch, I had heard a shout, the first sound I'd heard since the blackness had overwhelmed me: "We have his head out."

Oh, so I'm not dead, I thought, and then I passed out.

Later, as we neared the hospital, I heard someone say, "You can cut the siren now."

Our house happened to be on a hill from which we could see part of Main Street, and we were close enough to the fire station and hospital that we could always hear the sirens. At home, before she learned of my accident, Donna had just finished taking a shower and was preparing for the celebration of our wedding anniversary that evening. She heard the sirens screaming in the distance, but after living there for six years, she had become quite accustomed to them. Of course, always curious, she would wonder what had happened. Our little company had installed two-way business band radios, and we were the only one on that particular channel. Our base station was right there in the kitchen, so when Donna was in that room, she was pretty well aware of what her men were doing. The radio began to crackle. I'm sure she thought at first, "Did I hear right … someone hurt?" It didn't take long for her to get the answer. About this same time our son Larry was heading toward the shop with some newly purchased parts when he heard the emergency broadcast.

Donna and Larry were almost to the hospital when I arrived in the ambulance.

Certainly, the doctor's news for Donna, Larry, and Mike was not reassuring. He told them that because of the severity of my injuries, he needed to operate as soon as possible; but because I was in shock, operating immediately was too risky. Despite receiving two blood transfusions, my blood pressure continued to drop. Finally at about ten o'clock the doctor asked for permission to operate because he feared losing me.

When the ditch collapsed, the falling dirt and rocks seriously scraped my back; broke my arm and pelvis; damaged my bladder; and drove my stomach up through the diaphragm, breaking some ribs and popping a lung. A shovel I was carrying ended up being pushed against my chest with such a force that its wooden shaft broke. The rescuers thought at first that I had been impaled. Thank God that it broke before the handle punctured my chest. It was no wonder that I couldn't breathe. I was also dehydrating, probably because of my internal bleeding. When conscious, I begged for water, but they couldn't offer me any. Nurses were trying to clean the dirt out of my mouth with little wet Q-tips. When I realized this, I shut my mouth on them and tried to suck the water out. I thought of the rich man who died and went to hell, as told in Luke 16:24.

> And he cried and said, Father Abraham, have mercy
> on me, and send Lazarus that he may dip the tip of
> his finger in water, and cool my tongue; for I am
> tormented in this flame. (Luke 16:24)

I'm sure that Jesus went through this type of thirst, too, only many times greater, when he died on the cross for that great sin debt of the whole world ... for my sin and yours. The rich man experienced this level of thirst and was willing to give everything he had for one drop of water, but it was too late for him.

The doctor told me later that when he opened me up, his thought was to pull up the sheet and roll me out. Everything was crushed so badly that he didn't think there was any hope. He told me that I had asked him several times to let me die. He couldn't understand that, because the majority of his patients in a life-and-death situation would beg and plead for him to save them. I have also had nurses tell me that there is a great difference in the way people meet death—some in terror, and some in complete peace. Well, I can witness for the born-again believers that they die well. Praise the Lord forever!

Earlier when I saw "the book" close, I thought that my life was over. It was two in the morning when a heart rate monitor warning went off. My heart had stopped. What happened next is absolutely beyond describing. I remember being completely satisfied. I was still floating in the glorious presence of God ... in a river of living water. The next morning when I awoke, I thought about how I was so blessed to have experienced heaven and to have returned. Though my body was crushed, between life and death my heart was singing praises to Jesus, my Lord. Flesh pain can't hold its own against the presence of Jesus. I suspect that Paul and Silas were not feeling pain when they were singing in jail.

> And when they had laid many stripes on them, they threw them into prison, commanding the jailer to keep them securely. Having received such a charge, he put them into the inner prison and fastened their feet in the stocks. But at midnight Paul and Silas were praying and singing hymns to God, and the prisoners were listening to them. (Acts 16:23-25 NKJV)

I do not remember having pain as I lay there awake. It was just His overpowering presence that made the difference. O how precious! Just think what heaven will be like, if God will let us taste a little bit of that river that flows from His throne while we are here. Think what it will be like when we get over there. These Bible verses come to mind.

> But as it is written, eye hath not seen, nor ear heard, neither have entered into the heart of man, the things which God hath prepared for them that love Him. (1 Cor. 2:9)

> For in Him dwelleth all the fullness of the Godhead bodily. And ye are complete in Him which is the head of all principality and power. (Col. 2:9-10)

I'll never forget my tenth day in the hospital when they put me in a wheelchair and took me down to the end of the hall where there was a window from which I could see outside. As I looked at the green trees and the mountains, it was like seeing the world for the first time and with tremendous appreciation for its beauty. I was in a state of completion in Christ that is impossible for me to describe. Certainly any reproach for Christ's sake, any trial, any suffering, we have to go through here is not worthy of even mentioning.

On the fourteenth day they moved me to the VA Medical Center because I didn't have medical insurance and bills were piling up. I had many visitors who knew me through our family business and I could see in their eyes that many thought that I wouldn't make it. They need not have wasted any pity on me. I was on the winning side, whether I lived or went to be with the Lord. When Mike dug me out, the backhoe tooth hit my arm at the elbow and had taken out quite a chunk of meat and skin; it would need a skin graft. My arm was broken although they never put a cast on it. Day after day for a month they would dress the wound. I suspect they thought I wasn't going to make it and that was why they weren't putting the skin graft on the wound. I thought maybe the Lord was going to take me home to be with him. With my pelvis broken in two places I was a pretty sorry looking thing. It was no wonder people looked at me as they did. I certainly wasn't going to walk out of this place for a while.

It must have been about the fortieth day when, I guess, my spirits were low that I commenced to lament to the Lord and said, "Why, God, didn't You take me home to be with You?" I had experienced a good life and, besides that, we had a good accidental death insurance policy. My wife would have been left in good shape and our children were raised. It is so precious when God comes close and it seemed like His spirit lifted my whole being up off that bed (not literally) and said, "Son, you don't even have a right to ask. You have been bought with a price. You are not your own." I thought, *Thank You Lord, I'll never ask again.* We have a God that will talk to us. He is so full of love and compassion that we need not be discouraged, but just call on Him. He wants to hear us. That is why He made us; that we might fellowship with him. I learned there is no problem that is too big or too hard that He can't fix it. Remember He tells us to cast our cares upon Him, for He cares for you and me.

I was in and out of the hospital that fall and winter of 1976. It seemed like I was healing even better than the doctors expected. They said I would always walk with a cane, but the Lord had other ideas. As I recall the cane was tossed after six months and today one would never guess that I had ever been hurt. All glory be to God.

I knew now what Jesus meant when He said in John 11:25-26, "I am the resurrection, and the life; he that believeth in me, though he were dead, yet shall he live. And whosoever liveth and believeth ..." I also believe that King David and I have gone through some similar experiences and aspirations. Now, in my old age, I am driven to share Jesus' power and glory regarding the times He has restored my body and spirit. This Scripture says it best.

> Now also when I am old and grayheaded, O God, forsake me not; until I have shewed thy strength unto this generation, and thy power to every one that is to come. Thy righteousness also, O God, is very high, who hast done great things: O God, who is like unto thee! Thou, which hast shewed me great and sore troubles, shalt quicken me again, and shalt bring me up again from the depths of the earth. (Ps. 71:18–20)

Dear reader, think about what you have read. If it would have been you in that ditch, would you have been ready? None of us has assurance of another breath. I can't see anywhere in the Bible where it is written that you will have another chance after death. Don't be like the rich man who lifted up his eyes in hell and begged for a drop of water. Jesus is that living water, and He says, "Come you that are thirsty; come and drink freely of this water of life that I offer you." Do it now. God apparently spared my life here so that I may be of more service. I had seen clearly that there is an end coming when we will be judged based on our life, or on Jesus' sacrifice. I experienced a touch of God's holiness in His glory and can share that with believers. *The bottom line is that there is a God and there is a judgment. However, there is no death for the believer, only complete satisfaction.*

With such a life experience I knew God had plans for me to share His love and power with others.

CHAPTER 8

Bob's Deliverance

Sitting there in his house trailer, Bob had just told the Lord that he couldn't make it on his own. He would have to go back and work for his old boss on the job that he had quit because of his convictions about the dishonest practices his boss expected from him in the repair business. Bob was a Christian, and the Lord was taking him through a real chastisement. What followed, Bob's deliverance, is the subject of this story. Bob was about to witness the fulfillment of a promise in Isaiah when he heard a knock on his door.

> And it shall come to pass, that before they call, I will answer; and while they are yet speaking, I will hear. (Isa. 65:24)

A few weeks earlier, Bob and I were recovering in the same hospital. Bob had a severe stomach problem, and I was the victim of a trench collapse that left me at death's doorstep when I had been buried alive. We were in a hospital ward where we could see each other. I knew his name and face because of the small business I had run in our town. As time went by during our slow recoveries, we began to know each other and develop a friendship. He shared his problems of a bad smoking habit, which he knew he had to quit. But, as most every other addicted person feared, he believed it would be hard to break. He was carrying a heavy load.

In order for you to understand the whole story, I have to take you back a few years. My wife and I had met some missionaries who went to Alaska to preach to the fishermen, or boat people, in the summer. In the winter, they would come back to South Dakota and would stop by. It was always a wonderful time of fellowship. One day, they called and told us they needed to buy an outboard motor for their boat in Alaska, and they wondered if we could help. Our money was the Lord's, and we were glad for the opportunity to be of assistance. We helped them purchase the motor, and it blessed their ministry, but ten years later God spoke to them and told them to send the money back to us. Not knowing what God's plan for the money was, they just obeyed Him and returned the money.

By this time, Bob and I were both out of the hospital. We ran into each other at the post office and spent some time sharing how things were going. I could see that Bob was really emotionally beaten up and discouraged. The Lord spoke to me and said that I should give Bob a couple hundred dollars. By the way, we were not loaded with money and had some huge medical bills, so I prayed, "Lord, make my wife feel the same way about helping Bob." As I told my wife the story, mentioned what the Lord wanted me to do, and named the amount I was hoping to give Bob, she said, "Let's add that larger amount of money the Alaskan missionaries sent back." Of course I was delighted to hear her say that, as we were both on the same track.

That afternoon I took a check to Bob. After knocking on the door, I handed him the check and told him that the Lord wanted us to do this and he didn't have to pay the money back. We had asked God's blessing on the money and hoped that it would cover what was needed. Although Bob had the idea that men never cry, a tear slid down his face as he said, "You just saved my bacon."

"Well, it wasn't me," I explained. "All the glory goes to God."

Six months or so later our phone rang one Sunday afternoon; it was Bob. He wanted to come over and see us. As he came in, he handed me a check for more than we had given him. He said God had so blessed him that he could afford to do this. Then he said he was going to go into full-time Christian ministry. The money that I was going to give Bob would not have been enough, so God worked through those wonderful missionaries to meet the need. Yes, before Bob asked, God already had answered. What a wonderful God we serve. How wonderful it is that God reaches out to others through believers. Could it happen again in my life?

CHAPTER 9

Is There a God?

At some time during their lives, everyone asks themselves, "Is there a God? Does He answer prayers? Does He care about me as an individual?" As you have read in the preceding chapters, He has answered my personal prayers for deliverance in miraculous ways. As in the case of Bob's deliverance, this story demonstrates, in an undeniable way, how God answers prayers before they are even voiced. The story involves a barren cow, a Christ-centered farmer (me), and a missionary couple who needed a miracle to continue their work.

When we were first married, my wife and I rented my father's ranch. We were young and thought we had the world by the tail, but we had no idea how difficult life could be in South Dakota. A hailstorm could destroy our crop in a matter of minutes. During the Dust Bowl years, crops were lost for lack of rain, fences were covered by dirt, and at times locusts were so thick that they blocked the sun. We learned that our firstborn, Larry, had a heart defect at birth, and we mourned the loss of another of our sons, Wayne Allen. Yes, it was tough for us, and we asked God the tough questions. What are we here for? What is this life all about, anyway? And, is there a God?

In my youth, Mother had seen to it that we kids were taken to church—against our will. We thought that we had better things to do. The Bible says that God will not let His Word return to

Him void, but that it would accomplish what He wanted it to do. At the time, going to church and hearing God's Word seemed to be a complete waste of time to me and my siblings; however, the lessons we learned back then served their purpose, as I will explain.

You may remember my account of November 2, 1953, as I was driving a truck down the road and things came to a head. I was desperately discouraged about life in general, and I began to talk to God. I said, "God, if you are real and if You made this world and created everything in it, then surely You can talk to me. I want to know, I really want to know, if You are there."

Yes, I soon had the answer. I believe Jesus spoke to me, and He said, "Bruce, I died in your place to pay your sin debt; only believe!" Now, again, when Jesus spoke to me in the truck that day, it was much more than a thought. Whether it was audible or not, I really don't know, but I do know without a doubt what He said. He said it clearly in such a way that my spirit accepted his words and I was completely in love with Him. Somehow He gave me faith to believe. Although I didn't realize it at the time, I later understood that the Holy Spirit entered my soul to dwell with me forever. I was so filled with the love of God that at times I just cried with unspeakable and overwhelming joy. There was such a tremendous change, but I can only tell part of the story. I had a two-pack-a-day cigarette habit, and that was now gone. My filthy mouth was cleansed, the swearwords were gone, and love filled me so completely. It was real. It happened to me and entirely changed my life. Things turned around; now I love the things of God, which I used to hate, and I hate the things that I used to love.

> Therefore if any man be in Christ, he is a new creature: old things are passed away; behold, all things are become new. (2 Cor. 5:17)

Often because of that love and joy, I would sing praises to the Lord as I would do jobs around the farm. It is on just such an occasion that this story begins. On the South Dakota ranch, our summer pasture was twelve miles from where we lived. In the spring we would drive the cattle to pasture, and then in the fall we had a cattle drive, bringing the cows home for the winter months. I would go down to the pasture at least every week or ten days to see that the fence was up, if there was trouble I could fix with a cow, and so forth. As I was looking the cows over, I came to one that was the picture of health. She had fed on good summer grass that made her hide shine. She was likely barren because she had not had a calf that spring, and I knew that she would not be profitable this year. It would have been extra work to do anything with her at that point.

Even now, I think I could take you to the very spot in the field that I was working in when the Lord spoke to me. In a second, God told me in the same manner as He did before, in the truck, to take that barren cow, sell her, and have the check sent to the Guatemalan missionaries who had been at our church a few months earlier. I was so filled with joy that the God of the universe would speak to me that I responded as directly as I could. We had not known of this ministry prior to their being at our church. God knew them and was meeting their need.

It took me a while to carry out the plan, because the folks at the sale barn only held sales every two weeks in the summer. As I recall, it took me about ten days to take a horse down to the pasture, find the cow, and take it to the sale. I wanted to do this anonymously and thought I had, but I found out later it didn't work that way. The Lord worked out this detail as well, because if the missionaries hadn't known who had given them the money I had gotten for the cow, I wouldn't have heard what happened and wouldn't be able to tell this story. To God be the glory.

The sale barn had to have a bill of sale for the cow, and that information went on to the missionaries, so they did know who had given them the check. Having sold the cow, I went home and forgot all about it. Again, I don't remember the exact timing, but at some point later the missionaries came back to the States and visited our church once more.

At the beginning of the service, the wife half of the missionary couple gave a testimony, and here is what she said. The Guatemalan government told her and her husband that they had to pay a tax or else get out of the country. She said they didn't have the money. While she was out walking and pleading with God, she asked, "Lord, you called us here to preach the gospel, and now it looks like we are going to get kicked out of the country."

She said the Lord spoke to her and said, "The cattle on the thousand hills are mine."

She responded: "Lord, sell one of them." She said it was either that day or the next when she and her husband received a check in the mail for the sale of one cow. Oh yes! There is a God who loves us and cares. When the Lord spoke to me, these missionary folks didn't even know they would come to have a need.

> And it shall come to pass, that before they call, I will answer; and while they are yet speaking, I will hear.
> (Isa. 65:24)

CHAPTER 10

By Faith

In all things give thanks, for this is the will of God in
Christ Jesus concerning you. (1 Thess. 5:1)

No one knows the future, and it is a good thing that we don't. If
I would have known the pain that was to be mine this particular
day, I'm sure I would have just wanted to cut and run. This day
was the beginning of a couple of miracles that the Lord wanted to
show me.

I believe it happened in 1980 or 1981 when we had finished a good-
size pipeline job on Main Street and were starting work on a three-
day job in the country. This particular morning I was running a
wheel trencher. I've loved to operate equipment all my life, and you'd
more than likely find me operating something whenever I had the
chance. This particular machine had a winch right in front of the
operator, with a cable that would lift the big digging wheel. I suppose
that wheel weighed a couple of tons.

I had finished digging a short ditch and had moved over to a new
location. Even though I loved running equipment, it could be quite
monotonous to run this particular machine after it was set up and
the wheel was in the ground. As I was digging along, I decided to
stand up for a while. The cable that lifted the wheel by way of a
winch was right in front of me, and I would always grab it to pull

myself up out of the seat. I had on a new pair of leather gloves, and as I pulled myself up, the cable started to move on its own. The winch had a steel drum about eight inches in diameter. When engaged, it would turn, winding or unwinding the cable to lift or lower the big wheel as the operator desired. The clutch had been adjusted in the shop and evidently was set too tight. So when the oil heated up, the wheel just started on its own. Unfortunately, my unsuspecting fingers were caught between the cable and the drum.

Wheel Trencher

I guess because I was wearing the gloves, I didn't feel it soon enough to pull my hand out of the way. It had caught my glove and pulled my hand into the winch … One, two, three, four, fingers were drawn under that cable and severed. I thank God it didn't take all of my fingers but only the ends, including the fingernails. Of course the pain was so great that my brain was not able to work fast enough for me to reverse the winch in time to save my fingers. My first thought was, *This will pull me in and kill me.* At this time, even with the pain, I was actually filled with the joy of the Lord as I thought, *Lord, I will soon be with you.* My natural reaction was to pull, and after the machine had cut the ends of my fingers off, my hand came out of the glove, leaving my fingertips behind. About a foot of tendon had also been pulled out of my arm.

I was taken to the hospital and, due to the severity of the crushing and the tearing cut, the doctor decided I'd better stay there that night and he would try to straighten out my hand the next day. They had to take out the pieces of bone and get some kind of uniformity to the ends of my fingers before they could graft skin onto the tips. It left me with enough pain that I was on strong pain pills for several days.

I bet some of you are thinking, *Hey! This guy is just prone to accidents.* I do not believe in accidents. Jonah was not accidently swallowed by the big fish. "Now the Lord had prepared a great fish to swallow up Jonah" (Jonah 1:17). The Bible says that God directs the steps of a righteous man. Accidents? No, no, *no!* The Bible says, "In everything give thanks, *for this is the will of God in Christ Jesus concerning you*" (1 Thess. 5:18; italics mine). At times like these, you wonder why, but God is way ahead of you. Because I had this injury, the Lord gave me a number of opportunities to witness to people (nurses, engineers, suppliers, and others) about His saving grace that I otherwise would never have had. Was it worth it? Oh yes, many times over.

God is the potter, and He knows how to make a vessel out of us, fit for His use. The vessel (you or I) doesn't ask the potter, "Why are you making me this way?" God knows what He is doing, so instead of complaining, let's give Him thanks and praise that He saw something in us that He could use for His glory, for we know that "all things work together for good to them that love God, to them that are the called according to His purpose" (Rom. 8:28).

Our farm had done well financially through the summer, and I really didn't care if we did too much more work that fall. The only thing was that my foreman, who was my main help through the summer, would be out of work. We appreciated this young Christian man with a family, so we wanted to keep him on.

The day after I was hurt, a bid for a job we could do was coming up in the next town. Should we win the bid, it would keep our men busy for quite a while. That next afternoon, I had the foreman come up to the house to help Donna and me figure what our cost would be for this upcoming job, which was to be awarded that night at seven o'clock. The different supply companies always send out price quotations, so we already had the material costs but had to figure other expenses such as labor, permit fees, and profit. Keep in mind that I was on pain pills and was really out of it as far as figuring anything out. About five o'clock, Donna and my foreman came up with a figure and handed it to me. I had already asked the Lord to intercede for us concerning this job. For a couple of minutes, I looked at the figure that they had given me. Then I wrote another bottom-line figure under "Total Costs" and told them to make the total contract cost equal my bottom-line figure. They got their figuring done just in time for the foreman to take the bid over to the next town for the bid letting at 7:00 p.m. It was about 7:15 p.m. when the foreman called with great excitement in his voice. On a nearly $100,000 contract, our bid was $91 under the next bid. Was this a miracle? Yes, I'd say so. *To God be the glory.* With my being on pain pills and not being able to think clearly, I'm sure that I couldn't have come up with an intelligent bid ... but God wanted us to have that job to keep His children employed.

Since I wasn't feeling too well and had to have time to get used to my injured hand, I pretty much left the job in the foreman's hands. Possibly too much so, because as spring came near, we were supposed to be done at a certain date or else be subject to a $250-a-day penalty until we were finished. As spring approached, my hand had healed, but we were getting into a bind about having the job completed in time. I was able to get back on the job and speed up progress, but not as much as necessary. There came a time when we needed a miracle. I had seen the weather report the night before, and it said that we were going to get as much as a foot of new snow. I went to sleep that night in peace, not worrying about anything. Well, the next morning, business began to pick up. We lived up on a hill, and it was my practice to pull the drapes, drop on my knees, and pray. As I looked out, I saw a strong weather front coming. Being a pilot, I had learned something about the weather. The clouds were pouring in from the Gulf of Mexico, and it was easy to see that they were loaded with moisture. Getting a foot of snow, would not be uncommon this time of year. As I looked out, I threw my hands up and said, "Lord! What are you doing?" We just couldn't tolerate that much moisture and get our job done in time to avoid a penalty. Could God do another miracle? Yes, we have a God that can do anything.

Now, you might ask, "Who does this guy think he is, asking God to change the weather?" But the prayer of Elijah moved God to change the weather.

> Elijah was a man with a nature like ours, and he prayed earnestly that it would not rain; and it did not rain on the land for three years and six months. (Jas. 5:17)

The disciples said that Jesus was the Master of the wind. He calmed the storm. My prayer was answered and it didn't rain or snow for three weeks. We finished the job without penalty and traveled on down the road of life rejoicing in our loving and enabling Savior. God showed up over and over again in our lives to answer prayers. We need not be ashamed to tell of God's power in our lives.

Pipe-Laying Problems with High Soil Moisture

CHAPTER 11

Delight Thyself in the Lord

> Blessed is the man that walketh not in the counsel of the ungodly, nor standeth in the way of sinners, nor sitteth in the seat of the scornful. But his delight is in the law of the LORD; and in his law doth he meditate day and night. And he shall be like a tree planted by the rivers of water, that bringeth forth his fruit in his season; his leaf also shall not wither; and whatsoever he doeth shall prosper. (Ps. 1:1–3)

Why should we go around disgruntled and discouraged about life when God has shown us how to walk? God wants us to be delighted, and when we are, the Lord uses our joy to help others who are not delighted. The more you use this tool that the Lord has given you through His promises in His Word, the more delight and happiness you will have. There is no end to it. Not only that, but the Word says that you will be blessed. There is no end to the blessings of God toward His people who will delight themselves in Him regardless of the circumstance.

Remember the two disciples who were going up to the village called Emmaus after Jesus had been crucified? They were sad of heart as they walked alone, most likely thinking that it was all over, as far as Jesus was concerned. They somehow thought that Jesus was to be the earthly king and rule the nation, but now He was gone. The Bible says that as they walked along, Jesus drew near to them and walked with them, expounding to them all the Scripture concerning Him. As Jesus did this, their hearts were burning inside them, but they didn't understand why until later when He opened their eyes and they recognized Him. It truly is one of the greatest delights that we can have on this earth, when Jesus comes and opens our minds to His Word.

He even states that He will give us the desires of our heart. When we are in His Word, there is a real change in our desires. Of course we all think that the Lord should give us a million dollars, a new car, etc ... The reality is that when we are saturated with God's Word, those kinds of desires take a backseat, and we find that we are more interested in our neighbors and the lost souls around us. We begin to think, *Do they know Jesus as their personal Savior? Are they lost and going to the Devil's hell?* Then our prayer is, *What, Lord, would You have us do to win these people to You?* When we get to this place, the Lord will lay a real burden on our heart for them. We will pray and lay this burden down at Jesus' feet; and see Him work in those lives. Remember that Jesus said to bring our burdens to Him.

In Matthew 11:28, Jesus said, "Come unto me, all ye that labor and are heavy laden, and I will give you rest." Jesus is talking to the reader here. That means you and me. Remember, He already went through everything that could possibly come our way, so He knows how to comfort us and help us. He told us to be careful of the surfeit of the world; the cares of life can overtake us.

These days, one might have the responsibility for an elderly loved one, of being a single parent, or of having a sick family member with catastrophic medical bills. When we begin to be overcome by our worries about these things is the time to delight ourselves in the Lord. Listen to the following Scripture.

> For the weapons of our warfare are not carnal,
> but mighty through God to the pulling down of
> strongholds. (2 Cor. 10:4)

Many times Satan would like to overthrow us by way of our own imaginations. Whenever we are left in the dark for a while about anything—e.g., *Why aren't the kids home? They should have been home long before*—immediately the imagination will run away. *Oh, they have probably been in a wreck or kidnapped, or are even dead.* Our imaginations can soon develop a desperate, wildly despairing situation. If not checked, these thoughts will lead us right on down the trail of not trusting the Lord. The Devil loves to get anyone he can in this type of situation. But as Christians, our delight is in the Word of God, and we meditate on it day and night. So if we have been delighting ourselves in Him, we will have the weapons of warfare that will give us the victory, even over our own imaginations. Good, good news.

Remember how the Devil took Jesus out in the wilderness to tempt him? Jesus, being who He was, could say no to Satan on every score. We can also reject Satan, because Jesus lives within our hearts. Jesus used the Word of God when He said, "It is written, Thou shalt not tempt the Lord thy God," and immediately Satan left him and angels came and ministered to Jesus. This is the thing that we as Christians need to learn and practice. The most powerful weapon that we have is the Word of God. Many times the test or temptation seems like it is too strong for us to handle, and on our own it is. David understood the power that is in the Word of God when He said, "Thy Word have I hid in my heart, that I might not sin against Thee." The Bible says to resist the Devil and he will flee from us. The Word is so powerful that Satan won't just walk away from us, but he will flee or run. Isn't that great? Praise God. All glory be to the most high God of our salvation.

Memorize the Scripture so you will have it when Satan attacks you; hit him with it, and you will see Satan flee from you. There is no greater delight for me than to know that Jesus has sent Satan on the run and given us victory over him. After the Lord gives us victory over the Devil, the ministering spirits come and serve us. If Jesus our Lord needed them, certainly we, since we are no greater than our Master, need them even more. It's a time of rejoicing over the victory that our Lord has given to us. Praise His holy name!

Let's look again at what Jesus said: "I will give you the desires of your heart." What a promise! My desire, Lord, is to be more like you, to be filled with your Spirit of love and compassion for others, Lord, that you might always be on the throne of my heart, and that I might never submit to the sins of the flesh, or do or say anything that would displease you, and, Lord, that I might be a tool fit for your use. That my selfish pride of life, and all the ungodly attributes in my life, might be destroyed. And, Lord, please help me to win many crowns as I go through this life, for, when I see you, Jesus, it will be the greatest privilege of my life to cast them all at Thy feet, for Thou alone are worthy! I love you, Jesus. My desire, Jesus, is for you to be my king, and I will be your slave forever.

One evening as I was reading the Word before retiring, I received a special blessing from God. I was reading where the Lord said, "I was in prison and you came to me." It was one of those times when the Spirit draws near in a very special way and speaks to the heart. Two weeks after the Lord had told me to minister to the jailbirds, the phone rang. It was the Assembly of God minister, a real man of God. He wondered if I would take the jail ministry, as He was really busy about the Lord's work. God heard his servant's call for help and told this man to call me. We didn't go to his church, and very seldom did we see him, but I had great respect for him and his walk with Jesus. His call didn't surprise me. I tell this story to bring attention to how Jesus has complete control of communications. Not by phone, e-mail, or word of mouth, but *by His Spirit*. People usually use words to communicate between themselves, but there is no barrier to Jesus' ability to communicate with and between His people. To me, one of the most wonderful parts of my relationship with Him is that Jesus invited me to come and be bold. The temple veil that separated God from His people has been torn (Matt. 27:51). Now you and I are welcome to bring our thoughts directly to Him. He says, *I love you, come on in and let's reason together about what's on your mind.* I think He says, *Trust Me; tell Me how much you love Me; I love to hear how thankful you are for what you have received.*

Sometimes our physical problems become our spiritual burdens as well. Here again, God has come through for me.

CHAPTER 12

Walking with God

There is something about being mobile that is so precious. We should acknowledge how wonderful it is to be able to physically walk, run, and play without pain. Some of us go through life in wheelchairs or using walkers, and some of us, worse yet, can't even get up on our own. My heart is renewed with thanksgiving when I see a person who has a handicap getting out into the world, knowing how precious it is for him or her to do that. I believe we can compare the freedom to move about to the bondage of sin and death. The Bible tells us how to freely receive the most wonderful gift that one could ever get ... the Spirit of the Lord Jesus.

> And you *hath he quickened*, who were dead in trespasses and sins; Wherein in time past ye walked according to the course of this world, according to the prince of the power of the air, the spirit that now worketh in the children of disobedience. (Eph. 2:1-2)

All this leads to my telling you of a miracle that the Lord gave me, concerning my being able to walk without pain. My back had been hurt earlier, whether at the time I was buried alive or at another time, I just don't know. Anyway, a vertebra, about the seventh one up from my tailbone, had been pushed out of line. It was enough out of alignment that it was easy to see. Whenever I would bend over or straighten up, it would snap and hurt ... not unbearable, but somewhat painful.

My wife and I, then retired, were spending the cool summer months with our daughter in Washington State, to get away from the terrific heat that was at our new home in Arizona. My daughter's house was a split-level. The day of the miracle, my grandchildren were painting the walls on both sides of the steps. They had put a plastic liner on each side of the stairs and left about eighteen inches of exposure to the carpet in the middle to walk on. I was upstairs and decided to go downstairs, carrying an open can of Pepsi in one hand and a glass of ice in the other. Everything was fine until about eight steps from the bottom, when I happened to step on the plastic covering. My feet went out from under me and I was headed for the bottom. Never thinking of trying to brace for the fall, I was holding the soda and glass high so as not to spill any and make a mess.

Well, I landed on about the third or fourth step from the bottom. As I lay there in pain and shock, I thought I would probably be a paraplegic for the rest of my life. I was already in my early eighties, and we hear so many stories of seniors breaking a hip or a leg during lesser falls. My daughter announced, "I'm going to call nine-one-one."

"Oh no! Don't do that. I will be all right," I said. I could move my toes and everything seemed to be working, so I got up. Yes, my back was sore for a few days and there was a dark bruise around that vertebra; however, it no longer stuck out. As I fell down the stairs that day, Jesus had my hand and caused me to fall in such a way that the vertebra hit on the edge of a step and was pushed back into place. In this, He gave me a gift of healing. The bone had miraculously been pushed back into place, and, praise the Lord forever, it didn't snap with pain anymore when I bent over or straightened up.

I'm nearly eighty-seven now, and it is still in place. God works sometimes in mysterious ways. He is the Great Physician. I'm thinking it might have been quite an operation for a doctor to do what God did in an instant and in quite an unusual way. There is one who can save the vilest sinner, heal every broken heart, and fix every part of the body that might be broken.

CHAPTER 13

Cats, Cats, Cats

Living in Arizona, the wife and I were blessed by having a daughter who lived in Tacoma, Washington. So in the summer when our Arizona neighborhood would get up to 118 or 120 degrees, we could go up and live with her in the cool Pacific Northwest. I guess we were true snowbirds. Anyway, my daughter had three cats, and I had time to observe them. I think I saw some similarities between their lives and ours. Each cat had its own place in the hierarchy. The house we lived in was at the end of a cul-de-sac, and we could see the street and cul-de-sac very well. I noticed that when some of the neighbors would go out to get their mail, the alpha cat (the boss) would meet them with her tail held high. Well, now, how could a cat lover not reach down and pet her? This ended up being an open invitation for the cat to follow the person home and—I think in most cases—receive a treat. You see, the boss cat weighed about eighteen pounds. She would go around the neighborhood checking out her territory, marking it, and letting the other cats know she was boss. I think everybody in the neighborhood had one, two, or three cats. I guess it was her size that kept her queen of the block.

Now, it seemed like the three of my daughter's cats got along fairly well, except on some mornings we'd find some loose fur in the house; whether that was the result of enforced discipline or just play, I don't know.

I really wanted to have a little garden in the backyard, but it seemed like every cat in the neighborhood wanted to help. That nice soft dirt was more than they could resist. The way they would tear it up, one would think they were trying to help, but it turns out they were just using it as their latrine. It was disheartening to me, but it made for happy cats. There was a catch pond on the next lot, and through the summer the green plant growth came up and made the perfect hunting ground for those cats. One would be surprised at what all they would catch and bring home.

Every afternoon between two and three o'clock my daughter would open a special can of cat food, creating an anticipated little party for the cats. One cat seemed to hunt more than the other two, and many times that cat wouldn't be there. With some cats, the wishes of their owners are of secondary importance ... such cats possess a streak of independence.

My daughter would step out onto the balcony and call, and the cats would soon appear. One day I sat there at the kitchen table and watched this party take shape. As my daughter was opening the can of food, all three cats sat silently and just looked up at her and watched. They didn't move, meow, or do anything. They just sat there as if they were worshipping her. They knew what was coming. Two of them ate the solid part of the food; one would eat only the gravy. They each got what they wanted. Those cats loved my daughter so much that they would bring her presents, anything from a rat to a bird or a snake. You can imagine the confusion that overtook the house when these gift offerings were still alive. The cats brought what they had. This was just their nature; they couldn't change it if they wanted to.

As I was saying, I noticed a similarity between cats and humans, although God doesn't leave us humans like the cats do. When we look up to Jesus, we recognize that we are living in sin and we are not worthy of what He is preparing for us. Oh, we don't mess with snakes, rats, etc., but in some form or another God sees that we are living in the filth of the world. Satan has provided many things for us to wallow in. The Word of God says that all have sinned and fallen short of the glory of God. Once in a while, like on Christmas and Easter, we might go to church and, like the cats, try to give God a little something to pay for our ungodliness for another year. Wow, what a farce. I know we don't bring rats and snakes, but the unrighteousness that we do bring is about the same. Our soul is the only thing we have that is of any value at all. The Bible asks that if you gain the world and lose your soul, what does it avail you? All the treasures you collected become dust again, but your soul is eternal. You know Jesus doesn't ask for your money or what have you; He wants your heart.

Now this is what Jesus wants you to do: come as you are. You can't change yourself anyway, so come with all your sin, your hypocritical life. Bring it all. Don't try to hide anything from God; He even knows your thoughts. He said the following:

> Come now, and let us reason together, saith the LORD: though your sins be as scarlet, they shall be as white as snow; though they be red like crimson, they shall be as wool. I will in no wise cast you out. (Isa. 1:18)

How many of you have said, "Oh, the good that I have done will outweigh the bad"? Now, the offerings the cats brought in didn't change how much my daughter loved those cats, but she had to get rid of the offerings that they thought were so wonderful. The Word of God says that all have sinned and fallen short of the glory of God. So, *Come now,* Jesus says, *I will not throw you out, but we must take care of that filthiness you have.* God put our sin on Him (Jesus).

There is another comparison that we could make between humans and cats, but perhaps not with kittens: that of pride or indifference. Jesus said to come even as a little child, with believing faith; we are saved by grace through faith ... not by anything else. When you tell your child that you are going to do something, he or she simply believes you—and that's the way of salvation. *Only believe.* Your salvation can only be accomplished through Jesus. If you don't have faith, do like the man did when he asked Jesus for a miracle. He said, "Lord, help Thou my unbelief," and the Lord did. It seems like it is so hard for people to humble themselves and say, "I need help." It is nothing but pride that keeps us from humbling ourselves, so let's humble ourselves and admit we need help! Dump that pride and you will see the most wonderful miracle that can happen—your salvation. At this point, we can forget the cats, but we must not forget our situation. The Word says the following:

> Who knows the spirit of the sons of men, which goes upward, and the spirit of the animal, which goes down to the earth? So I perceived that nothing is better than that a man should rejoice in his own works, for that is his heritage. For who can bring him to see what will happen after him? (Eccl. 3:21-22 NKJV)

> For God so loved the world, that he gave his only begotten Son, that whosoever believeth in him should not perish, but have everlasting life. (John 3:16)

> For whosoever shall call upon the name of the Lord shall be saved. (Rom. 10:13)

> But as many as received him, to them gave the power to become the sons of God, even to them that believe on his name. (John 1:12)

> Therefore if any man be in Christ, he is a new creature: old things are passed away; behold, all things are become new. (2 Cor. 5:17)

This is what Jesus will do for you. You will find that now you love the things that you used to hate, and you hate the things that you used to love.

Yes, those cats will keep on hunting for snakes and rats, but in Christ, you and I have been made into *new creatures*. With our new hearts we don't go hunting for the filth of the world. God's Word says to abstain from the very appearance of evil. Obey the new Spirit of Christ that is in you, find a good church and godly people, and read the Word of God. Best of all, you can talk to God now. He wants to hear from you. He is on His throne making intercession for us every day. He will never leave or forsake you. Whatever the burden might be, Jesus is able to lift it and deliver you from it. Lay it down at His feet and be free! Jesus said, "Let us reason together."

CHAPTER 14

Is There Hope?

We need understanding and enlightened before we can do much of anything. A cook can't just throw any ingredient into a pan and hope that a nice cake or meal will come out. A mechanic can't overhaul a motor without first having some understanding of a motor.

We will not just by chance fall into heaven when we die, any more than that mechanic will get a motor overhauled just by chance. Have you thought about what heaven will be like? It will be full of people praising and worshipping the Lord. Ironically, that would be a form of hell for the unbeliever. Many have spent all their lives avoiding God's children; the church of which Jesus is the head; and the Bible. We know unbelievers would not be comfortable in heaven. They will not be comfortable in hell, either. The fact is that they are headed for an eternal disaster. The good news is that God will help you avoid the eternal disaster. In His wisdom, He has instructed His people in how they should try to help you.

> And a servant of the Lord must not quarrel but be gentle to all, able to teach, patient, in humility correcting those who are in opposition, if God perhaps will grant them repentance, so that they may know the truth, and that they may come to their senses and escape the snare of the devil, having been taken captive by him to do his will. (2 Tim. 2:24–26 NKJV)

Notice that last sentence. The unsaved are caught in the Devil's snare, and the Devil is able to make them do anything that he wants, according to his will. Here is why the unbeliever can't comprehend.

> But the natural man receiveth not the things of the Spirit of God: for they are foolishness unto him: neither can he know them, because they are spiritually discerned. (1 Cor. 2:14)

Perhaps you are playing a charade like the people I told you about earlier who wanted me to mark their hands in the palm when they came into the dance hall, so they could go to church the next day and no one would be the wiser. I wasn't even a Christian, but as I marked them, I was nauseated. What must God think of this kind of charade? The truth is it's like Alta, told me: "Bruce, you can know that if you should die, your sins are forgiven and you're ready for heaven."

Thank God, I found it, and you can too. This is life and death that I'm talking about. We are going to spend eternity someplace. It will either be in heaven with our wonderful Lord and all the saints, or else it will be in the lake of fire with Satan and all the lost. God's Word says that there will be weeping and wailing and gnashing of teeth in hell. I don't say this to scare anyone. It is only reality.

This is where the spiritual birth comes in, without which we are blind as bats to the spiritual things of the Bible. In John 3.3, Jesus tells us, "Verily, verily, I say unto thee, except a man be born again, he cannot see the kingdom of God." Then He goes on to explain what He is talking about in verses 5 and 6: "Verily, verily, I say unto thee, except a man be born of water and the spirit he cannot enter into the kingdom of God. That which is born of the flesh is flesh; that which is born of the spirit is spirit."

He is talking about two different births. We all know that our first birth was in water; we came from our mother's amniotic sac. That is what Jesus is telling Nicodemus about. So that leaves another birth that we have to deal with—the rebirth of our hearts (and mouths). There is no other way.

> "And ye shall seek me, and find me, when ye shall search for me with all your heart. And I will be found of you," saith the Lord. (Jer. 29:13–14)

Remember that Satan is bidding for your soul and that he is the Father of Lies. Why wouldn't he use lies to keep you his slave?

I remember when Jesus came into my heart. One of my first thoughts was, *How simple, why couldn't I have caught on sooner?* The Devil had planted a false idea in my heart that salvation was so hard to receive that it really was unattainable for me. The Devil is a master liar; don't let him deceive you on this point.

The truth is, and it couldn't be any simpler, that you just need to believe from your heart—without any reservations. Repent and admit to Jesus that you are a sinner, simply ask Him to come in and take over. Tell Jesus that you want Him to do the driving from here on out, that you will get in the backseat. Do it now. Don't wait; right where you are, ask Him in. The Word says that today is the day of salvation. We do not have a lease on life. We just don't know whether we have even another minute. I was driving a truck when Jesus came into my heart. No matter where you are, *believe* and ask Him now. If you did what I just asked you to do, then you are born again, and you should thank Jesus for coming. In the days ahead, you will see your desires changing. The Bible says that if any man be in Christ, he is a new creature, old things are passing away, behold, all things become new. You will find yourself loving the things that you used to hate, and hating the things that you used to love. You will find yourself loving God like you never knew was possible. You will have a deep love and compassion for the lost, and you will have a deep interest in the Bible. You will be surprised how much better you understand it now that you know the author.

You have a new Master now; listen to Him and obey Him. He will lead you into all truth. Go find a good church of which Jesus is the head. Go regularly and worship the Lord. You will find that the Lord has many people who know and love Him. You are part of the family of God now. Welcome to the family.

Jesus said, "Freely you have received, freely give!" Share with others what He has done for you. From now on, do what Samuel told the children of Israel to do in 1 Samuel 12:24: "Only fear the LORD, and serve him in truth with all your heart: for consider how great things he hath done for you."

About the Author

Bruce Blair was born in 1926 in Geddes, South Dakota. He is a Navy veteran, having served in the South Pacific during World War II. Shortly after being married, he became a farmer with his wife, Donna; they took over the family farm. He started Blair Pipeline, Inc., in the 1960s, and in 1975 he sold the farm to focus on his pipeline business. He retired in 1986 and started to winter in Arizona. He moved there in 1990. In the 1990s he started to write down the many things that had happened to him over the years so that his grandchildren might come to know God and how he had loved Him. Not only has Bruce had these inspiring life experiences, but he has also explored his artistic talents as a wood sculptor. While some of his works have been sold, many still adorn his home. When a farmer, Bruce became a pilot and has since logged hundreds of hours in command of several kinds of single-engine aircraft. He and his wife of sixty-five years now live in Maricopa, Arizona, with their daughter, Elaine.

Acknowledgments

First and foremost, I want to acknowledge Jesus Christ, my Savior, for demonstrating His love and direction in my life to make this writing available so that every reader might understand His grace a little better than they had before. Also, I wish to thank all of the following people who were so willing to give their help in making this testimony available. These people include my wife, family, and several friends who encouraged me to get the stories down in writing. Many years later after the project all but died, I met Lee Murray, a Christian and a retired snowbird, who, after hearing one of my stories, also felt that they should be shared. Lee gave new life to the project. He had some writing experience and felt led to facilitate the publishing of my book. Lee solicited the help of other Christians in this effort.

CPSIA information can be obtained at www.ICGtesting.com
Printed in the USA
BVOW071324300613

324651BV00001B/2/P